CONSENSUALITY

HOW TO LOVE OTHER PEOPLE WITHOUT LOSING YOURSELF

T0027131

CONSENSUALITY

HOW TO LOVE OTHER PEOPLE WITHOUT LOSING YOURSELF

Helen Wildfell

MICROCOSM PUBLISHING

PORTLAND, OR ⚥ CLEVELAND, OH

Consensuality: How to Love Other People without Losing Yourself
© Helen Wildfell, 2015, 2023
First Edition, First Printed, April 1, 2015
Second Edition, First Printing, February 2023
This edition is © by Microcosm Publishing, 2015, 2023
Cover illustration by Cecilia Granata
Edited by Lex Orgera
Book Design by Joe Biel

For a catalog, write or visit:
Microcosm Publishing
2752 N Williams Ave.
Portland, OR 97227
https://microcosm.pub/Consensuality

ISBN 9781648411205
This is Microcosm #192

To join the ranks of high-class stores that feature Microcosm titles, talk to your local rep: In the U.S. **COMO** (Atlantic), **ABRAHAM** (Midwest), **BOB BARNETT** (Texas, Oklahoma, Louisiana), **IMPRINT** (Pacific), **TURNAROUND** (Europe), **UTP/MANDA** (Canada), **NEW SOUTH** (Australia/New Zealand), **GPS** in Asia, Africa, India, South America, and other countries, or **FAIRE** in the gift trade.

Did you know that you can buy our books directly from us at sliding scale rates? Support a small, independent publisher and pay less than Amazon's price at **www.Microcosm.Pub**

Library of Congress Cataloging-in-Publication Data

Names: Wildfell, Helen, author.
Title: Consensuality : How to Love Other People without Losing Yourself / by Helen Wildfell.
Description: [Second edition] | [Portland] : Microcosm Publishing, 2022. | Summary: "There are infinite possibilities in human relationships, but the fairytale ideal of companionship does not exist for most people. In Consensuality, Helen Wildfell and her co-adventurers detail the process for creating or finding a healthy, successful relationship as well as common pitfalls and how to avoid them, like gender identity, sexual boundaries, power struggles, and emotional dysfunction. Overcoming regret and resentment, the authors describe a journey towards a respectful social environment. Their experiences lead to lessons of self-empowerment and communication tips for building healthy partnerships. We recognize their preferences and boundaries. We discuss how those fit with our own preferences and boundaries. Filled with personal descriptions of the complex layers in human interaction, the book combines gender studies with memoir to truly make the personal political"-- Provided by publisher.
Identifiers: LCCN 2022014636 | ISBN 9781648411205 (trade paperback)
Subjects: LCSH: Interpersonal relations. | Intimacy (Psychology) | Respect for persons.
Classification: LCC HM1106 .W54 2022 | DDC 158.2--dc23/eng/20220328
LC record available at https://lccn.loc.gov/2022014636

MICROCOSM PUBLISHING is Portland's most diversified publishing house and distributor with a focus on the colorful, authentic, and empowering. Our books and zines have put your power in your hands since 1996, equipping readers to make positive changes in their lives and in the world around them. Microcosm emphasizes skill-building, showing hidden histories, and fostering creativity through challenging conventional publishing wisdom with books and bookettes about DIY skills, food, bicycling, gender, self-care, and social justice. What was once a distro and record label started by Joe Biel in a drafty bedroom was determined to be *Publisher's Weekly's* fastest growing publisher of 2022 and has become among the oldest independent publishing houses in Portland, OR and Cleveland, OH. We are a politically moderate, centrist publisher in a world that has inched to the right for the past 80 years.

Global labor conditions are bad, and our roots in industrial Cleveland in the 70s and 80s made us appreciate the need to treat workers right. Therefore, our books are MADE IN THE USA.

TABLE OF CONTENTS

INTRODUCTION _____

CHAPTER 1: DYSFUNCTIONAL CYCLES ____

Breaking Down the Cycles _____

    Cycle 1: Bad Habits as Coping Mechanisms _____

    Cycle 2: Unresolved Resentments _____

    Cycle 3: Unhealthy Sexual Interactions _____

Reflection Questions _____

Practice Action _____

CO-ADVENTURER: A Competition of Some Sort: Dysfunctional Ideas

CHAPTER 2: RETHINKING PATTERNS _____

Early Influences and Seeking Therapy _____

The Language We Use _____

Destructive Behaviors _____

    Behavior 1: Self-Harm _____

    Behavior 2: Substance Abuse and Coercion _____

    Behavior 3: Avoiding Emotions _____

Reflection Questions _____

Practice Action _____

CO-ADVENTURER: Ebby, or Through Pinnochio's Looking-Glass __

.... 10

.... 18

.... 28

.... 28

.... 29

.... 32

.... 35

.... 36

at a Relationship Should Be 37

.... 48

.... 48

.... 57

.... 61

.... 61

.... 65

.... 69

.... 75

.... 76

.... 77

CHAPTER 3: TACKLING GENDER ROLES ____

Resentment Towards Men _____

Learning to Be Myself _____

Struggling with Masculinity _____

Reflection Questions _____

Practice Action _____

CO-ADVENTURER: Schrödinger's Dick: It's Yours, It's Beautiful, and It

CHAPTER 4: ESTABLISHING BOUNDARIES _

Why Boundaries Are Important _____

Boundaries and Abuse _____

Maintaining Boundaries _____

Reflection Questions _____

Practice Action _____

CO-ADVENTURER: Diligence + Battlements _____

CHAPTER 5: EMBRACING CONSENT _____

From Pressure to Assault _____

Learning About Consent _____

Creating Safe Spaces _____

    Discussion within Communities and with Sexual Partners _____

    Embracing the Spectrum _____

Reflection Questions _____

Practice Action _____

THE FINAL CO-ADVENTURER: You! _____

....95

....95

....99

....103

....107

....108

ugh 109

....123

....123

....124

....131

....134

....136

....137

....158

....158

....157

....160

....160

....167

....171

....172

....173

INTRODUCTION

*C*reating happy, consensual relationships is a complicated endeavor. When you care about people, you are forming a complex bond that develops through layers of varying perspectives and boundaries. Generally, when we as humans begin sexual relationships, we don't know everything about our partners' perspectives. We learn more about each other as relationships progress. Your partner(s) will have triggers and boundaries that aren't obvious from initial interactions, and the same will apply to you. You may not even understand your own triggers and boundaries yet, but that's okay. Boundaries and triggers vary from person to person and will be informed by many influences—from family judgements to brain chemistry differences to major traumas to plain old personal preferences.

Consensuality is a form of sensuality that is deeply entwined with consent. It is the process of building respect and consent, not just in sexual interactions, but in all aspects of relationships. It means being proactive about discovering what you and your partner(s) need to feel healthy and happy in a relationship. It means going beyond the simple structure of "yes" or "no" in the traditional definition of consent, and sensing when you or your partner are uncomfortable. In the past, I often said "yes" in sexual situations even when I didn't want to have sex because verbal communication during sex wasn't enough for me and my past partners to truly establish consent. True consent can only be enacted when everyone involved is comfortable with the situation and able to freely and truly express yes or no.

I wrote *Consensuality* to help you navigate all of the complexity, messiness, and misunderstandings, working towards more healthy, consensual relationships.

Before we begin, the first thing to note is that this book focuses on romantic and sexual relationships. All healthy and consensual relationships are good—they don't need to be romantic or sexual to be valid, but the experiences in this book tend to focus on the issues involved with sexually intimate relationships. If you are asexual, you may still find value in the book as many of the healthy habits that apply to sexual interactions also apply to other interactions. But, unfortunately, this book is not a good fit for anyone who isn't comfortable reading about sexual experiences.

Throughout *Consensuality*, in chapters that explore dysfunctional cycles, patterns, gender roles, and boundaries, I will share my own experiences and directly address you, the reader. The motivation behind this style of writing is to establish a conversation between us, rather than a formula for you to follow. When it comes to relationships, there is no direct map towards perfection. The beauty of this is that you don't have to agree with everything I say to find meaning in the book. This book is about you finding your own way, and sometimes your path will look different from the experiences I describe.

While a person can be violated in many types of situations among couples, acquaintances, friends, family members, or strangers, my experiences with consent (or lack of consent) tend to focus on long-term romantic relationships. In my own journey, I've noticed that consent can deteriorate when people in long-term relationships expect sex and/or build resentment towards one another, and for me, the lack of respect was often influenced by gender stereotypes.

In order to build healthy relationships, it is important to recognize that we all experience the world through a subjective lens informed by our own background and experiences. I intentionally included sections by other authors, or co-adventurers, throughout the book to expand the types of experiences included and reinforce the fact that we are subjective individuals. The reality is that my own perspective combined with how I am perceived by others causes me to focus on particular issues. My writing stems from my own observations of unequal power dynamics

in relationships, and I emphasize how gender and sexual interactions affect mental health in relationships. It is very likely, however, that someone with a different background (or even a similar one) could find an alternative approach to gender and sexuality within the context of relationships.

My acceptance of my own subjectivity is why this book also proposes that all people should have an equal right and opportunity to express their needs within feminism as a movement. I do not want *Consensuality* to contribute to the false narrative that white feminists can represent all feminists. I understand the need for some to distance themselves from the word feminism because the movement has a history of ignoring the perspectives of people of color. Just as it was unfair for the white feminist movement to ignore other perspectives for decades, it would be unfair of me to assume that I could somehow create a universal guide to feminist relationships. While this book is meant to help people avoid the lack of consent that I experienced in some of my relationships, I know that experience looks different and at times will be more difficult for different people. My hope is that you as the reader will consider your own identity as you read this book so that you can use my experience as a springboard to finding your own process for forming healthy and consensual relationships for yourself.

Before beginning *Consensuality*, examine your perspective. Explore what you want from yourself and others. Really dig deep. It is time to go far beyond what you want in a partner. Explore who you are right now and what you want for yourself. You may come from a privileged background or you may have been subjected to many injustices. You may value independence or perhaps you are looking for additional support.

At the end of each chapter, I will include reflection questions and a practice action in order for you to explore your own perspectives on the topics covered in this book. You can use the questions as journal prompts, meditations, conversation starters, or however else you see fit. Reflecting on our experiences is an important first step towards understanding ourselves. Without practice, however, we won't be able to put our

new discoveries into action, so follow through by experimenting with the practice action. Each practice action will provide a simple way to apply the lessons learned in each chapter.

Ask yourself these reflection questions now:

- How do I see myself?

- What is my view of my own gender and sexuality?

- How do my views on gender and sexuality affect my relationships?

- Do I feel comfortable in my current relationships?

- Where is my starting point in this journey?

And then, follow through with the practice action below:

Invite someone else to join you on this journey. They don't need to be a romantic or sexual partner, just someone who will be supportive. There are some heavy issues in this book, so having someone else to discuss these topics with can provide accountability and insight through the process. And, even if the person says no, that's okay! That is well within their rights, but the act of asking is (1) a very important lesson in consent and (2) a chance to open up about your own journey.

My hope is that this book will act as a caring friend for you as you find your own path towards consent. Names have been removed or changed to protect everyone described in this book. Continue the consideration by taking care of yourself and others while reading through these pages. Consensuality contains discussions on many issues that require care to properly process, including sexual assault, substance abuse, and attempted suicide. Go slow and don't hesitate to stop and reflect. While this book is primarily focused on romantic and sexual relationships, consider how all of your relationships — friends, family, lovers, or any other co-adventurers in your life — relate to the personal experiences in this book. Use reflection and action to discover your own consensuality.

CHAPTER 1:
DYSFUNCTIONAL CYCLES

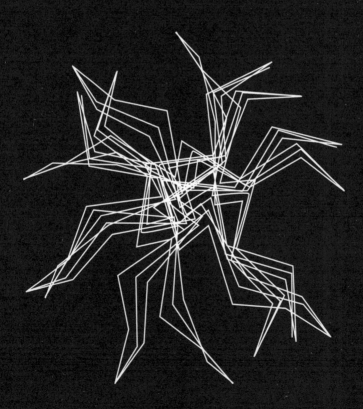

An Unhealthy Bond

For the first twenty-two years of my life, I tried to deal with my relationship issues on my own in a way that I perceived to be "logical." When a relationship went bad, I would jot down any of my own psychological damage in need of repair as if I were compiling a to-do list for myself. An example of one of these lists is copied below. This list was taken directly from a past journal:

- My compulsive need to always say "sorry"

- My inability to be assertive

- My lack of control

- My resentment towards men

- My fear of rape

- My association of sex with rape

Journaling was a great first step towards recognizing my personal issues, but I tended to stagnate there. When I looked back on lists like the one above, the end result was always me feeling bad about myself. Instead of looking at my own

issues as part of a larger puzzle, I just felt fear. My issues felt insurmountable. Although my concerns were legitimate, I was concealing them from other people and misunderstanding their root causes. I was not learning how to resolve these issues in my relationships. My frustrations remained hidden in my journals until my inability to express these feelings oozed into my daily life.

Even as a child, I felt anxious about these issues, and I misunderstood their sources. I remember walking home with my field hockey stick in middle school and thinking, "Well, at least I have this giant stick to use as a weapon in case a man attacks me on my way home." Let me be very clear, I was not sexually assaulted as a child. I wasn't dealing with any direct sexual trauma. I was simply reacting to the news stories from my childhood that heavily covered instances of girls and women being raped and murdered by strangers. These news stories combined with gender stereotypes created further misunderstandings about how men and women interacted with one another. As a teenage girl, I simultaneously craved and feared relationships with men. I wanted the romance portrayed in movies, yet I was also convinced that men would use me for sex. All of these misrepresentations of gender created an incredibly unhealthy starting point for forming intimate relationships.

After years of misunderstanding my feelings and fears, I ended up in a long-term monogamous relationship that was not going well. My boyfriend and I argued frequently, usually about drinking, sex, or both. We had moved in together within four months of dating, and I quickly discovered that my boyfriend drank daily. About once a month, we would have a big blowout fight because of something he did while he was drunk. He needed help with his addiction, but other than telling him that it bothered me, I had no clue how to get him the help he needed. We were what I viewed as a typical young couple—dysfunctional, with lots of ups and downs. I had no clue what to do. I loved him, but it was becoming more clear to me that being around him was negatively affecting me.

Among other things, my self-esteem had gone down the drain. I was never a super confident person, but any confidence I had was destroyed in the wake of our unhealthy dynamics. I struggled

with his comments towards me, especially when he was drunk. My family had noticed that he would talk down to me. Hardest for me, however, was that he would pressure me into sex or encourage me to drink alcohol to "loosen" me up. We were a mess, but despite our serious issues, we trudged forward.

About two years into the relationship, I wasn't ready to end it completely, but I decided to move out. By this time, I understood that something needed to change in our relationship, but I thought with some distance and independence that we might still be able to resolve our problems. I moved into a campus apartment where the level of respect was dismal. A poor, neglected guinea pig squeaked in the living room corner while my roommate and her boyfriend screamed at each other daily. I had traded my own bad relationship for a front row seat to another, but I tried to focus on what was within my control. I was attempting to build some sense of self-respect even if I was living in a chaotic environment.

To celebrate my new independence in my apartment, I planned to go out with two of my best friends. It seemed like a normal thing for a twenty-one-year-old to do. I told my boyfriend that I was going to spend time with friends that night. I didn't expect to see him. But my nights out with friends were always a source of concern for my boyfriend. He had a different agenda. Without telling me, he suggested to my friends that we pick him up and go to a bar closer to his house. I only found out about his plan once my friends were on their way to my apartment. I didn't want to create drama, so as usual, I went along with the change in plans.

When we met with him, he was already intoxicated, which immediately filled me with anger. When my boyfriend and I drank together, things often went horribly wrong. We began the turbulent night by arguing without resolution. I struggled to hold back my resentment, but after only five minutes, I needed to get away from him. I asked my friends if they wanted to go on a walk to get some food, thinking I could temporarily avoid further conflict. I was unaware that, according to my boyfriend, we would be wandering around a bad neighborhood. He snapped at me:

"Yeah, why don't you just go and get raped."

I didn't even think. Upon hearing the statement, years of resentment broke out of me, and I slapped him as hard as I could.

Silence followed; neither of us could process what had just happened. I had felt rage before in previous fights with him, but I had always been able to control my emotions. At worst, I would strangle my frustrations by screaming into a pillow. Now, all I knew was that I had reached my limit. He had crossed a boundary too many times, and in return, I regretfully admit that I had crossed a huge physical boundary by hitting him.

Later that night, delayed reactions continued to pour out of our bruised psyches. His frustrations flooded into further damage, which ended with him yelling at me repeatedly for being "fucking stupid." My friends yelled back in response and then rushed me out of the situation, disturbed by what they had witnessed.

My friends took me back to my apartment. We talked for hours about the complications of my relationship. They showed me that there were people who respected my thoughts and feelings, even if I didn't know how to respect myself yet. I felt very ashamed and small at that moment. I had stayed in a verbally abusive relationship for years as my self-esteem deteriorated. Most disappointing to me was that I had now physically abused him.

My boyfriend showed up with flowers and chocolates the next day. I refused to talk to him, so he left the items on the doorstep. Noticing the gifts, my roommate remarked how I must have a sweet boyfriend. But presents could not explain how to stop hurting each other, nor could they undo the damage that had been done. The alcohol had erased most of his memories of the night, and I stored the information for ammo in future fights. Neither one of us was properly equipped to maintain a healthy relationship.

Chances are you've witnessed or experienced similar situations in your own life. Dysfunctional relationships are all too normal. When I told other friends about the fight, some people told me that it wasn't a big deal to slap a man, and when I heard other stories about men in drunken mishaps, "boys will be boys" was a common explanation. It was easy to lean on gender and relationship stereotypes when they allowed us to justify our actions. The whole situation could be normalized, from the hurtful things he said to the physical abuse I inflicted.

So, what could I do? It wasn't as simple as getting out of the relationship, which felt nearly impossible. Self-esteem issues ate at both of us. Insecurities kept me within the confines of the relationship, isolated from others. On the other hand, his fears seemed to be expressed through alcohol use and attempts to control his surroundings. I often attributed his problems to his excessive drinking, but distrust also continued to develop when he encouraged me to drink. In between sober affection, drunken sex was normal for us. Unwanted sex was normal for me. The emotions of our dysfunctional relationship were cyclical, pushing and pulling away from each other. We had been in the cycle for so long it felt natural to go back and forth between anger and love.

As a result of our unhealthy bond, the relationship lasted much longer than it should have. Every couple months or so we would have a big blowout fight followed by promises to be better. It only ended completely two years later, after I gradually found the tools to care for myself. Even then, there was regret to deal with after the breakup. I needed to examine everything I knew about myself if I hoped to create healthy relationships in the future. I had to understand the sources of my shame and resentment before I could discover confidence. This meant exploring the internal problems that I had shelved my whole life, spanning from issues with my family to societal views of gender roles. The night I hit my boyfriend, I began a complex search for something that I couldn't understand yet: consensuality.

Breaking Down the Cycles

Like many people, I only sought help after I was already in trouble. I was reacting every step of the way rather than being proactive about communicating my values and concerns. My initial blindness and denial of my issues within the relationship contributed to these unhealthy cycles.

Cycle 1: Bad Habits as Coping Mechanisms

To start, my boyfriend and I each brought plenty of bad habits to the table. In my view, the worst of his bad habits was excessive drinking. Drinking is a common means of avoiding negative feelings. It can also be used as a way of self-medicating for mental health issues. But, unlike therapy and prescribed mental health medications, alcohol doesn't help resolve any of the underlying issues that lead to low self-esteem, depression, or any other number of mental health issues. Often within our relationship, alcohol actually exacerbated his self-esteem issues, but because he would forget so much once he was sober again—including the negative feelings and the drunken fights—it was difficult for him to understand why drinking was a problem for him.

On the other hand, I had the bad habit of internalizing my negative thoughts and feelings. I had no problem expressing positive emotions even during times when internally I was feeling depressed. Part of the reason for this was that I valued pleasing others above my own feelings. At one point, when I really wanted out of the relationship but was afraid of how it would make my boyfriend feel, I told myself that I would never be with anyone ever again if it meant that my boyfriend could just move on with his life and be happy with someone else. I remember expressing this sentiment to a friend, who bluntly told me that it was an insane thought, but my bad habit of people-pleasing had made the situation seem reasonable. My boyfriend and I were both using these bad habits to cope with our own issues instead of addressing them head on.

Cycle 2: Unresolved Resentments

Lingering in our bad habits, we thought we were masking our issues from one another, but really we were just hurting each other over and over again. We could get by day to day, but our resentment towards one another increased bit by bit. All of the

pain without any way to process it turned into huge resentments until finally one or both of us lashed out in anger. Our escalating frustrations came out in brutal ways, the fight described at the beginning of this chapter being only one example of our destructive actions. Combined with our unhealthy coping habits, the fights just led to more and more resentment. We would eventually make up after our fights and be better for a bit, but we never truly addressed the core of our own individual issues.

We would often avoid our resentments by creating more physical space between us. I stayed with my mom and stepdad frequently. I didn't think of it this way at the time, but the weekends when I would visit my mom were essentially giving me a break from our relationship. On his end, he would go on long tours with his band, giving him the opportunity to travel around the states. The tours also gave him the opportunity to drink without it escalating into a fight. If we had been aware at the time of how we were using physical space, we might have been able to harness that coping mechanism to think on our issues and then revisit them together to find solutions. The problem is that, instead of taking time for ourselves and then addressing the issues between us, we just used the space for avoidance. Eventually, I became resentful of how long he was gone. I'll admit that some of it was envy. I would have loved to travel too, if not with him then at least on my own, but I had a full-time job that didn't allow me that kind of freedom of movement. I don't know what his thoughts were on me leaving for many weekends, but I do know that I was very resentful of how he could pick up and go for weeks at a time.

Looking back on how resentful I was towards my ex, I can clearly see that we both had a lot to work on individually. I believe that if we had been healthier individuals, we would have realized a lot sooner that we weren't compatible. We were frequently irritated and hurt by each other, yet we continued to force the relationship for a total of four years. We were obviously attached to each other, but ultimately we couldn't find a way to respect each other. Instead of working together as partners, we oscillated between fights and resentment.

Cycle 3: Unhealthy Sexual Interactions

Of all of the negative cycles in my prior relationship, to this day, over ten years later, the hardest part for me to write about is our unhealthy sexual interactions. For one, we were together for four years, so there's a lot of history, and it all feels muddy and messy. From the beginning, our sexual relationship was unhealthy. As someone who wasn't very good at expressing myself, I wasn't talking to my boyfriend or anyone else about the issues I was experiencing during sex, but I knew that sex was often physically painful for me. There were and still are some positions that make sex less painful for me, me being on top being one of them. Unfortunately, there are also positions that made sex more painful for me, in particular "doggy style" (a phrase that still makes me cringe). This position, of course, was the only way that my boyfriend could orgasm during sex. Add onto this the major issue that my boyfriend did not like using condoms. It should have been very obvious to me that these were major problems.

My unhealthy way of dealing with these major problems, however, was simply accepting them as just how it was. For the vast majority of our sexual interactions, I would start on top until I orgasmed and then we would switch to doggy style until he came. We would also generally start having sex without a condom until he got close to orgasm when I would ask him to put one on. Looking back on this, I can see from a mile away that this was never a good solution to our sexual issues. We didn't communicate about sex, and we had no plan to talk through these issues. At one point, we went to counseling and when the counselor asked us about our sex life, we both brushed it off like it was fine.

• • •

Unhealthy cycles are hard to recognize when you are in them. Or, even when we recognize the cycle, we may not know how to break it. This wasn't my first serious relationship. I had been in a long-term relationship before and, unsurprisingly, I had the same bad habit of not expressing myself clearly in that relationship. The only difference was that my previous boyfriend, to his credit, broke up with me when things started getting really dysfunctional. He saw what I could not admit, that I needed to work on myself. But I hadn't matured and grown

enough to change the cycles yet. I was still afraid of being alone, and I was afraid of what breaking up with my boyfriend might do to him. I was afraid of confrontation, of recognizing our issues. But, because this dysfunction wasn't created overnight, it also wasn't fixed overnight. I had to work on myself before I could break unhealthy cycles within my relationships.

Dysfunctional cycles are not limited to dysfunctional people. Remember that just because you've been in some bad relationships, it doesn't mean that all of your relationships are doomed to be the same. But I won't sugar coat it, forming healthy communication takes work. You will get frustrated with other people. It happens to all of us. You may want to explode in an outburst or hide in a hole when conflict arises in your relationships, but recognizing your tendencies and how they contribute to dysfunctional cycles is the first step.

If you are currently in a romantic or sexual relationship(s), take this moment to recognize your priorities and concerns within your own context. Recognize that this is just as much your relationship as it is your partner(s)' and that your concerns are real. While you can't control other people's actions, you are capable of forming healthier communication habits for yourself. Wherever you are in your relationship journey, our goal in this book is to aim for healthier interactions before situations escalate into additional harm, but to do that we must first address past issues. Whether you are in a romantic relationship or not, you likely have some habits and tendencies that have caused communication errors for you.

Consensuality, you will discover, is different for different people. Ask yourself the reflection questions and practice the action listed below. Can you begin to recognize behaviors and patterns that create unhealthy relationships? Ultimately, the answers you've always been looking for in relationships are obtainable through healthy reflection.

Reflection Questions

- What are some of your own unhealthy habits that you've noticed during your interactions with other people?

Examples include "the silent treatment," yelling, drinking excessively, etc.

- Have any of your own unhealthy habits reappeared in multiple relationships? If so, how?

- Are / were any of your unhealthy habits exacerbated by interactions with a romantic or sexual partner?

Practice Action

When you're ready, express a concern that you've had in your own sexual interactions to someone. Express this concern to your sexual partner(s) if you are currently sexually active, or share this experience with someone else that you are close to. Opening up to my husband and some close family members about how I experience pain during sex has helped me find solutions. For one, lube! For two, non-intercourse sexual interactions! These are two very simple solutions that my husband and I have had fun exploring because I was finally able to open up about my experience.

A Competition of Some Sort: Dysfunctional Ideas of What a Relationship Should Be

M. Izen

Because he is a trans man, I expected things would be different from the usual fuckery I was resigned to dealing with in my previous relationships. And it was, at first. I hoped that a compassionate, authentic understanding of the bullshit women endure on the daily would create a space where none of the typical inequalities would exist. I thought of him as a sort of unicorn—one of a kind, special, super smart, feisty, and fearless. We had a great connection that was really fun with tons of laughter. I loved having sex with him. Our friendship ripened pleasantly, we had known each other for many years and had a super comfortable and sweet friendship.

One day we arrived back from a hike and both needed a shower. I was renting a small place so there was nowhere for him to wait for me but on the bed. It seemed awkward for him to just sit and wait while I took a shower, and we had been friends for so long that it actually seemed less awkward to just take a shower together. I said, "You can just take a shower with me if you want." He hesitated, so just to let him know that it was no big deal, I stated the obvious and shrugged, "You don't have to if you don't want to." His face lit up and he grinned and jumped up, "Yeah, I want to!" I thought it was so funny and cute.

One of my favorite things about him is how brave and fearless he is, not afraid to ask for things or have an adventure. It was true, he did realize, understand, and embody issues unique to women. It was fun to dish and bitch about old white men and the patriarchy with him, and that was such a refreshing departure from relationships with clueless men who were authentically trying but just didn't have the perspective to truly get it. On the other hand, I suspected that this was also an inner struggle for him. He had spent his entire life identifying as male, faced with a world that was rife with problems instituted by "old white men." For the first time, in his ripe middle age, he began to embrace a bit of his female identity, something to which I had always known him to be vehemently averse. I admired and respected his fluidity. It was genuinely refreshing. I found that I was much easier for me to tolerate certain qualities in him that I hated in cis men, ones that I found to be unattractive or undesirable. They just didn't present in the same way for him. I found I much more generously offered some grace that I was not so likely to offer to the partners of my past. Old rules did not mean anything in a context that had no context, no previous experience, and no rules or standards based on gender expectations. Some of that ease came from the evolution of our friendship. We were comfortable with one another; we were having a great time.

So, we were friends first and lovers last. I've never understood why we can't seem to afford our romances the same grace that we afford our friendships. We cut our friends a break; we overlook their faults; we forget about it when they stand us up, without scrutinizing excuses or looking for nefarious deception; we support them through the tribulations and struggles we would call deal-breakers and grounds for divorce in a romance. There was a moment before our friendship blossomed into a disaster when, out of genuine adoration, he said to me enthusiastically, "Hey, I love you!" as one would to a friend, and I responded emphatically and without hesitation, "Oh my god, I love you so much!" I threw my arms around him in the biggest heartfelt hug. Why does this interaction look so different in the context of romance? Who should say it? When? How to respond? As soon as the friendship entered into the realm of a partnership, it was doomed almost before it began.

The joy we felt for each other shifted and descended into dysfunctional ideations of what this new scenario *should* look like. We both abandoned our best selves within a comfortable friendship for an imitative toxicity with no other blueprint but destructive pain. We dragged the nasty corpses of past relationships out to the present and to one another. Because that was all we understood and were seemingly capable of, neither one of us was able to access anything better. We both knew better. We knew how to be good people, we just didn't know how to be good partners, and as soon as that line was crossed, everything went to shit. I still don't know what happened. I'm still

super confused. Was it me? Was it him? I mean, the obvious answer to both is yes, but I'm left to wonder what part of it was fought and destroyed in my head. What began as friendship turned briefly and blissfully intense, only to descend into a toxic ephemeral mess.

Suddenly everything became an opportunity for friction. He refused to get vaccinated for COVID-19 although he had lung problems his entire life. This presented as a real trigger for me from a past relationship where I had watched someone literally deteriorate as they dabbled and flirted with conspiracy theories that I perceived as extremely toxic and destructive. Although I found the refusal to vaccinate disturbing, what I found even more upsetting was his participation in the negative narrative fueling this decision. Although I wanted to respect his privacy, I was concerned about the toxic disinformation stew he was immersing himself in and how it might affect our interactions. Per usual, he was not willing to claim or admit to these as held beliefs, making it difficult to pinpoint if it was a problem. I'm of a "you do you" mindset, but I felt that spending time in this

nefarious space seething with negativity would only produce more of the same, and it did. This was a departure from the person I had known in the past, a person I had often described to others as someone with the best attitude of anyone I had ever met. Much of that was still there, but there was also so much negativity and dwelling in constant complaints as conversation. Much of this resonated as a general acknowledgement of social justice failures, but at the end of the day, it manifested as a constantly negative rhetoric without solution. I felt like he was including me in an everything-that-is-wrong-with-the-world scenario and inhabiting a dark place where the world is dismal and stacked against everyone.

He had, earlier on, expressed to me that he was in a sad place; he was upset by a relationship that had soured. He looked at the ground, shook his head, and said, "I'm mean to my girlfriends," something I should have perhaps paid more attention to and that he later denied. But, because I heard it, I looked for it and anticipated it coming.

It's easy for me to say where he was wrong; it's harder to place what my part was in all of this. I'm sure he would have a totally different rendition of our relationship. We tried to talk things out with some success, but things had gotten uncomfortably antagonistic, and it was hard to turn that around. Those blemishes were always lingering somewhere, and everything from that point felt tarnished. A shiny, excited spark devolved into a strained, forced fix. It's always hard to recover a relationship once things begin to deteriorate.

Exacerbating the situation even further, the typical corruption of mutual reciprocity morphed into a power struggle. Financial disparities are so commonplace yet forever so problematic. Like many others, we fell victim to the resentment of unequal financial contributions. He was super comfortable taking but not so much with giving back. Financial disparity tipped the balance and created tension. My lack of clear financial boundaries created problems. I will always choose to pay rather than have it be an issue, without understanding that that, in and of itself, becomes an issue. It seemed like everything turned into a power struggle, a competition of some sort, because he couldn't resist the opportunity for a competitive clash. He became suddenly contrary for no other reason than a perversion of romance. If I had an idea, he had a better one or would dismiss any knowledge I might have or advice I might offer. Suddenly it became exactly like all of my past failed partnerships. All of our concerns became bigger issues that snowballed.

His style of reciprocity would be to cook me a meal full of the precise foods I said I preferred to avoid, as if to make the point that I was ignorant of my own nutritional needs. He would force time and schedules. Even when he had no place to be, he insisted on me conforming to some arbitrary schedule to suit himself. He got agitated when I would not rearrange my schedule to accommodate his lack of one. He resisted when I appealed to him for easy reciprocity. Instead of seeing it as an opportunity to nurture a relationship, it was perceived as a forced obligation that threatened his autonomy without being able to see that he might water the plant to see it bloom. Instead, he acted like he was being coerced into obligatory chores that would resonate as weakness, and it perpetuated a resistance to participate in any other way than on his terms. He was painfully and awkwardly straining to make everything appear to be his idea. When he was reluctantly and uncomfortably reciprocal, it was never a question of what I would like or when I would like to do it, it was always I'm doing this, at this time, for you. Okay.

I descended into a toxically negative thought loop, I quickly became frustrated and uncomfortable with a dynamic that felt resistant, competitive, and judgy, and it ambushed my thinking. I was unquestionably having hormonal issues that I was well aware of and took responsibility for. I tried to use humor to soften and lighten the situation and grew angry and resentful when my self-deprecating humor was used against me. I knew this type of mindset only intensified and invented discord that would burn everything to the ground, but I couldn't seem to get control of the fire that threatened our fragile dynamic already teetering toward volatility.

I did the "womanly" thing. I took the responsibility. I accepted the blame. I thought somehow that it would open the road to move on and be done with it. Looking like a fool or flawed was less important to me than resolution. I just wanted to clean up my side of the street quickly and get it over with, even if I didn't necessarily think I deserved that. I thought that by accepting responsibility and blame it would open the door for him to come clean too; instead, it just tore open a wax-sealed invitation to blame as if I had conveniently admitted to the ultimate reason for the failure and the matter had been decided in his favor, a nice and tidy absolution for him. Because I cited emotional moodiness as a culprit, now everything was dismissed as something I was inventing in my head. He seized on the opportunity to let everything be my fault because it was too painful for him to acknowledge or even comprehend where he was also romantically toxic. It was convenient for him, and classic accommodation on my part. It opened the door for him to look for evidence of a forgone conclusion, one that would conveniently fit a narrative that I was somehow inherently flawed in some way that rendered me comfortably disposable. I was trying so hard to fix things to which he responded dismissively with a cavalier, "Hey, either it's fun or it's not" attitude but he was orchestrating resistance then blaming me when it wasn't "fun." In the end, the whole thing just imploded as a tragic reminder that although we were both otherwise well-intentioned people, we were seemingly mystified by the skills required to accomplish turning our spark into a flame that wouldn't torch us both to the bone.

CHAPTER 2: RETHINKING PATTERNS

Early Influences and Seeking Therapy

*I*f we rewind a little bit to the beginning of my story, finding consent within my intimate relationships was inextricably linked with family issues and mental health. You may find that your story is too, so we will start there. Even if you haven't experienced major problems with your own family and mental health, you have probably come across someone who is working through these things. Particularly when it comes to mental health, we must all work together to recognize the importance of accessing adequate care in regards to mental wellness.

Before I even recognized my own mental health issues, professional counseling was the first tool I used to explore my feelings in dysfunctional relationships. I wanted to examine why I regretted so many of my actions and feelings. I had grown up with the belief that there was some sort of cosmic balance to traditional gender roles, an idea I had inherited from my dad, so I was struggling with how I could be assertive as a woman. My family did not adhere to strict gender roles in the way that deeply religious or traditional households

might, but that's the thing, no one is immune to societal expectations. At this point in time, no one can completely escape the gendered associations that society imposes. Gender roles are embedded across families, cultures, and societies. In my family, we were raised with New Age beliefs, so instead of viewing gender roles as the laws of "god," we embraced femininity for women and masculinity for men as a necessary part of "finding oneself." There was a sense of empowerment in embracing womanhood, but that feeling still came with expectations for how a woman (or man) should act. Just being a person with unique wants and needs wasn't an option.

Later, involved in the previously mentioned dysfunctional relationship, I began to recognize that my notions of gender weren't working. I was being suffocated by my ideas of womanhood, so I turned on the person who taught me about the spiritual and social divide between men and women—my dad. In and out of counseling appointments, I complained about my dad often and wondered why I couldn't get over my issues. With good intentions, counselors often tried to remind me that my dad didn't have a manual for raising me, but all I could see was that my dad and society hadn't given me the right guide for my life.

Growing up, I struggled with regret and confusion over many of my decisions. I was praised for bending to others' wills, rather than holding to my own beliefs. I was the definition of a "people pleaser." Instead of confronting my issues, I learned how to navigate around them in an attempt to keep everyone happy. My dad would tell me that I was a "master of feminine energy," so it was ingrained in me that I was somehow better for fitting into the stereotypical passive gender role for women. I didn't try to expand outside of that identity because I didn't know there were other options. I thought I was fulfilling an innate role, but the end result was that I felt frustrated without the means to understand why.

My parents were self-proclaimed hippies. They watched as second-wave feminism emerged, witnessing major changes in birth control and reproductive rights that gave women more agency in their lives. My parents were liberal and open-minded when it came to religion, health, and

many social issues, but something was left behind. Even if my dad was comfortable with external social change, he still believed in the binary system that says women and men should have different roles in personal relationships. Masculine equaled aggressive and feminine equaled passive in his mind. Just like me, he learned these ideals from the people around him. Family, spiritual leaders, and his other sources of information echoed that there was a natural order to gender roles.

Your parents may or may not have been hippies, but they likely had some sort of beliefs surrounding gender that influenced you growing up. Gender roles can seem inescapable as a young person who is inevitably being guided by parental dynamics. Especially at a young age, it can be difficult to untangle the things we actually believe and want from the things we've been made to believe that we want. If we are told something over and over again, we are going to digest that information and believe it. As I became more aware of how my dad's beliefs had influenced me, however, I also realized that I no longer had to adhere to those beliefs.

My dad never questioned his beliefs about gender. He felt very comfortable expressing them. And, even if it wasn't always intentional, his beliefs surrounding gender were embedded in his actions. My dad would criticize women in his life who didn't fit into his definition of feminine. In particular, he judged my sister and mother for having strong, outgoing personalities. Learning from his reactions to the women in my family, I knew what would make me look better in his eyes. It wasn't until I was an adult that I started recognizing his criticism of women as problematic. As a child and teenager, I didn't understand that socialization within my family wasn't blatant. It was hidden in our day-to-day interactions. Most of all, I didn't realize that being socialized into a particular role could negatively affect my future relationships and create all sorts of scenarios that would lead to regret.

In addition to familial influence, up until age eighteen, I had very little understanding of any form of feminism. My mom taught me the importance of a person's right to reproductive health, but I had no idea how gender inequality

affected intimate relationships. Before I went to college, while I knew things didn't seem fair, I didn't have access to comprehensive education on any type of social justice. I was aware that people often viewed women as weaker, physically and emotionally, but I internalized many of those feelings instead of recognizing them as societal fallacies. As a result, I strove to be that girl that wasn't like other girls. I didn't realize that the problem wasn't being a girl, the problem was how society raised and judged girls. I didn't realize that by suppressing my own feelings, I was really just feeding into society's judgment of women and causing issues within my intimate relationships. It took years of nudging through dysfunctional partnerships for me to realize that patriarchal roots within our society allow many men to justify their dominant role in personal relationships.

Ultimately, counseling and education helped me unpack how both society's and my family's dynamics could negatively affect my future relationships. In anthropology and psychology courses, I learned about how people in general could be socialized into specific roles (and many of the things that I learned in college about socialization are now taught to students at a younger age), but more important than any courses, counseling helped me make the connections between societal and familial expectations and my intimate life.

As a result of counseling, I eventually felt comfortable speaking directly to my dad about how our family dynamics affected me. When I finally told him I didn't adhere to his views of gender, he still disagreed with me. He was adamant that most people innately fulfilled his gendered descriptions, but he accepted that I wanted something different. I couldn't control my dad's views, but speaking to him about my own beliefs and needs was huge progress! I had expressed my opinions to my dad instead of just absorbing his ideals. I would have never reached this point in my journey without the help of my counselor.

Hopefully you are way ahead of me and have already sought help, but if you haven't and you feel like you're floundering, seek help now. There is no shame in asking for help. And it can take time to find the right help—I had three counselors before I found the right one for me. The other counselors

still helped me along the way, but ultimately I needed a counselor who was looking at my actions through a feminist lens. My counselor empowered me to speak more openly and confidently in my everyday life. Finding the right counselor was the best thing I ever did.

Unfortunately, there are still major issues regarding access to mental health resources within our society, such as the high cost of mental health care and a lack of diversity in the counseling field. I was incredibly fortunate and privileged that as a college student I had access to resources. If you have access to counseling resources through your school, workplace, or another organization, use them. They are there to help you. But, if you don't know how to get access to counseling, start by using the resources below:

Substance Abuse and Mental Health Services Administration (SAMHSA) Resources
SAMHSA's helpline and online treatment locator offer free, confidential, 24/7, 365-day-a-year treatment referral and information (in English and Spanish) for

individuals and families facing mental and/or substance use disorders.

SAMHSA's Helpline: 1-800-662-HELP (4357)

Online treatment locator: findtreatment.samhsa.gov

The Boris Lawrence Henson Foundation

The Boris Lawrence Henson Foundation is a non-profit committed to promoting and offering mental health resources for the Black community.

borislhensonfoundation.org/mwsp-free-virtual-therapy-support

The Language We Use

Counseling wasn't a magic wand that fixed all of my problems. It only worked because it helped me face my issues and unpack them one by one. One of the first things I tackled was the language I used that ended up compounding instead of alleviating regret. With my counselor's help, I started unpacking my obsessive use of the word "sorry." Sorry was my favorite word for a long time. The first time I had a feminist counselor who actually

considered how people are affected by gender in their daily lives, she noticed this about me and helped me understand why I felt the need to say that I was sorry after every other sentence. She helped me understand why I felt regret so often.

"Sorry" is meant to express regret for something said or done, but I found myself saying it even when I didn't have a reason for regret, which created a whole different kind of regret. I accepted guilt for everything at the first sign of social discomfort. Even when I tried to express my opinion, whatever I said was frequently followed by "sorry." "Sorry" slashed through many of my expressions and feelings, often counteracting my justifiable emotional responses. I found so many ways to apologize for things that needed no apology. I would start sentences with "You're gonna hate me for this" if I was expressing an opinion or detailing an action that I felt the other person would disagree with. I realized my apologies weren't just excessive politeness—my language habits were affecting my identity, minimizing my confidence in my beliefs and actions.

I had been taught that being a woman meant navigating around conflict at the expense of my own feelings. Being "sorry" was the easiest way for me to dissolve disagreements. If I apologized enough, I thought I could move on. In reality, I was holding on to more and more resentment. After I would say sorry, people usually responded with, "It's okay." Most people accepted my apologies and probably thought very little about it, but internally I was constantly questioning myself. In my relationships, my emotions did not seem to matter as much as other people's feelings. Although I could express myself in private, sometimes in destructive ways, I often ignored my feelings in relationships.

Because of my constant apologies, I found myself developing unequal power dynamics in romantic relationships. Of course, some people recognized this and encouraged me to have more confidence, but with the wrong person, someone who would take advantage of my always being "wrong," my self-esteem would plummet. I needed to rewire how I spoke with my partners, and in turn, they needed to respect my opinions in our interactions.

Recognizing how my language was fulfilling gender stereotypes and decreasing my confidence was a big step towards feeling less regret. I began to understand that ultimately we are all socialized to interact with one another in specific ways, and often the type of socialization depends on the sex you're assigned at birth. No one is immune to this problem. One could argue that apologizing isn't even the problem in itself, instead the larger problem is that we have different expectations for how men and women are going to treat people. How we balance our own confidence and politeness towards others shouldn't be dependent on the sex we're assigned at birth. How kind and confident you are isn't dependent on your genitalia. We have the amazing ability as humans to expand beyond the expectations of gender stereotypes.

Noticing and recognizing our language habits can serve as an important starting point for addressing deeper issues. While language is not our only means of communication, it is obviously a huge part of how we share information with others. The words you use convey a lot to other people. This is why I'm not surprised that when consent first started becoming a societal conversation, there was a huge emphasis on using clear language to express "yes" or "no." Unfortunately, misunderstanding the intent, some people made fun of this by claiming it was equivalent to necessitating a contract before sex. But, the initial emphasis on clearly stating "yes" or "no" before sex was actually a recognition that our other methods for communicating during sex were failing. Emphasizing the importance of saying "yes" to sex was a huge step towards diving deeper into what it takes to truly create consensual sexual relationships.

Destructive Behaviors

Behavior 1: Self-Harm

It can be difficult to untangle who you are from what other people expect of you. Everyone has to deal with this issue on some level. Unhealthy emotional reactions like acting tough or playing passive are often expected based on our perceived gender. Combined with a history of mental health issues, this process was physically destructive for

me at times. I wish that many of my issues had been addressed before they reached the extent of physical harm, but unfortunately that wasn't the case for me. If you see or experience any of the harmful behaviors that I share in this chapter (or any signs that things are heading in that direction), you should seek help from a professional immediately, and know that if you have already experienced these issues, it is never too late to recover from them.

The least apparent of my destructive behaviors was the most damaging—physical self-harm. I had begun scratching myself when I was thirteen years old. At that age, I already thought women were more likable when they were passive, so my family and friends generally did not know when I was upset. Instead of approaching people for help, I mistakenly thought it was admirable to quietly hurt myself. Even into adulthood, the habit of physically harming myself continued. Self-harm was one of the few ways I knew of expressing extreme negative emotion.

When I moved across the country to Virginia for college, no one knew that I had developed this destructive habit. I became extremely homesick about a month into moving to Virginia, a situation that no doubt was exacerbated by a long-distance relationship with my first love. I would stay in bed all day because I had very few coping skills. So, when my depression reached an extreme point, I bought Tylenol with the plan that I would take enough to kill myself if I felt like I couldn't go on anymore. The worst part was that I knew that overdosing on Tylenol was a horrible way to go, but my depression was so extreme that hurting myself had become the priority. One day, when my depression became too much to bear, I overdosed, shocking the people in my life. Even I was surprised, as I was so numb that I didn't fully understand what I was doing. Thankfully, the positive relationships in my life, in particular my love for my mom, stopped me. I called my mom, who contacted the campus police. I was taken to the hospital where I spent the next twenty-four hours vomiting up Tylenol and receiving fluids. It was a nightmare.

The experience exposed my family to the emotions I had been suppressing, but no one should have to get to that point before receiving

help. Over the next several years, I received more support from my family, but my personal recovery was slow and intermittent. Though rare, there were still moments when I resorted to cutting and scratching myself. I now know that destructive behaviors can be healed through coping mechanisms, positive interactions, and professional treatment, which, for me, eventually included medication. I was so ashamed of my depression and anxiety for years, but a huge weight was lifted off my shoulders once I found the appropriate treatment. Finding the right tools and forming communicative relationships has been the greatest method for combating my own self-harm. Even if you haven't experienced thoughts of self-harm or suicide yourself, you likely know someone who has. Through communication, we all need to look out for one another and ensure people are receiving help when they need it.

If you are dealing with self-harm or thoughts of self-harm, know that the Suicide Prevention Lifeline is always there if you need it. Don't be like me. Reach out for help sooner rather than later. I always thought that it was better to handle my mental health issues on my own, but eventually I reached a point where I couldn't function. Now that I have received help for my own mental illness, I can't believe that I suffered in silence for all of those years. I feel more like myself than ever. Getting help was life changing, and my only wish is that I had sought treatment sooner.

National Suicide Prevention Lifeline

Available 24 hours, 7 days a week, 365 days a year in English and Spanish

Dial 988 anytime, anywhere. 988lifeline.org

Behavior 2: Substance Abuse and Coercion

Everyone copes with mental health issues in different ways. Unfortunately, sometimes we develop destructive habits, including self-medicating with harmful substances. For my ex-boyfriend, the man I regretfully hit, drinking was his dysfunctional comfort. He would drink nearly every day and binge on weekends. As mentioned earlier, drinking seemed to mask his self-esteem issues. Ultimately his story is his own, but I can speak to my own experiences with alcohol and how it affected me more than I initially realized.

Our mutual drinking habits affected me long after we broke up.

I always thought of drinking as his destructive behavior, not mine, but shortly after ending the relationship, I began making more trips to my favorite bar. If I had a free night, I was destined to end up there. Unintentionally, I gradually increased the amount of drinks I had in a night. Even if I had work the next day, the need to drink seemed too hard to resist. I had spent years coping with someone else's alcoholism, and now I was developing my own drinking habit. Drinking wasn't the issue in itself, but it was how I was using alcohol. It had transformed into an unhealthy coping mechanism.

I was fully single for the first time in four years. Despite finally being done with the relationship, I wasn't sure how to be single. Spending nights out drinking became my default. In addition, I discovered that drinking and sex had become intertwined in an unhealthy way for me.

The thing about my relationship with my ex was that I knew I felt uncomfortable with him sexually, but it wasn't like I could point to one specific time when he crossed my boundaries. The issue was the gradual wearing down: it was having to say no again and again, just to say yes out of exhaustion. It was knowing that he wanted me to drink because often that was the only way I would say yes to sex. It was the times when sex was physically hurting me, but he still wanted to continue. It was the compounding of all these experiences.

I'm not saying this is a legal version of sexual assault, and I definitely don't think we should send every person who pressures a significant other to prison. I don't believe prison solves anything for anyone. But we do need to reckon with how coercing people into sex, whether through the use of a substance or incessant pressuring, should never be normalized. It was normal for me. Throughout the relationship and afterwards, I struggled to process how these violations affected me.

Drinking lingered in my life, and when I started dating a new person, it became even clearer that I should not have sex under the influence of alcohol. I would crave pain during sex under the influence of alcohol, and not in a fun, kinky way.

I would lash out and all of the emotions that I usually kept inside would explode. Essentially, I was a mess sexually. I didn't know how to consent to sex because a lack of consent was normal in my previous relationship.

In the 2015 National Intimate Partner and Sexual Violence Survey, the CDC reported that 16 percent of women and 9.6 percent of men had experienced sexual coercion in their lifetime. (Unfortunately, the survey did not recognize non-binary as a gender.) Self-reported data always has some limitations, including possible hesitation from participants to share intimate information, but even if this survey data is completely accurate, we can still do better.

If we base our numbers on the survey, more than one in ten people have experienced sexual coercion in their life, meaning that you likely know someone who has experienced sexual coercion (possibly yourself). You may have dated someone who has experienced it. Or, you may have even intentionally or unintentionally coerced a partner into sex. It is an all too common experience that can cause regret and shame in a relationship. Be aware of both your own sexual past and your partner(s)' because these issues generally don't resolve themselves on their own. Discuss any concerns that you may have before you have sex. After experiencing dysfunctional sexual interactions with my ex, forming communicative and positive future relationships was crucial to my survival. I had to express myself in order to heal, and I needed people who would listen.

Behavior 3: Avoiding Emotions

To this day, I am still healing and understanding what works best for me and my partner. I had been ignoring my feelings for a long time, so unlearning it all proved to be a pretty difficult feat. Destructive behaviors often restricted my self-expression to private and painful moments. Like a hose with a kink in it, emotions flowed into me, but only a trickle would come out. Some people preferred for me to be passive, my feelings or wants rarely inconveniencing them. But, kept inside, my feelings and wants also couldn't help anyone. They didn't help me understand myself; they didn't help others understand me. Without regular expression of my emotions, my view of the world was very

limited. I overvalued restraint and saw others' emotional reactions as weakness. Out of fear that my own feelings might be exposed, I avoided interactions with people I perceived as emotional. As a result, my feelings became so restricted that it was painful. I would get depressed or angry when my own unexpressed emotions boiled over. I would go to counseling, but it was very difficult to begin expressing more emotions in my everyday life. I associated feelings with extreme moments of depression, such as when I overdosed on Tylenol. I felt guilty if I let more than a trickle out.

I wasn't able to express my feelings until it became more apparent that resentment and guilt were interfering with the positive relationships in my life. After a long dysfunctional relationship, I became pickier about who I allowed into my life. I sought people who were patient and kind, avoiding the stereotypical and superficial relationship games. I worked hard to only continue relationships with people who respected me, but I still had a hard time finding respect for myself.

When I began dating my current spouse, I felt extreme anxiety when he showed any dissatisfaction or simply went home for the night. I couldn't understand why I was so codependent, and I tried to ignore these feelings, but they would eventually culminate in panic attacks. The condensed anxiety generally lasted a few minutes, during which my brain flooded with fear. I felt as if I was going to die. My past regrets were doing all they could to push everything away. I couldn't continue to live with the unwarranted guilt from expressing my emotions.

Bursting with a need for outward expression, one of the first things I did was shave part of my head—something that I had wanted to do for years, but I had always been afraid of how people would react. My physical appearance became an important form of expression in my repressed emotional state. I was learning to present myself how I wanted, regardless of awkward stares and comments. This small step was the beginning of my realization that I had a right to express myself.

The next step in changing how I viewed my personality and emotions, however, was much longer and more significant. I started expressing my inner feelings. I openly told people that I

apologized too much. I noticed and removed unnecessary disclaimers from my speech. Small decisions like choosing a restaurant for a group dinner or saying no to people when I didn't want to go out became moments of empowerment. I shared what I wanted in big and little ways. After holding in my feelings for so long, I realized that feeling in the moment was the only way I wanted to live.

Anthropology, psychology, and gender studies classes in college helped me understand how society affects individuals, but college is a huge privilege, and in reality we should be teaching these things at a much younger age. Emotional expression and support in childhood and expansion beyond heteronormative and cisgender examples in primary education can give people the confidence to discover how their own identity adheres or differs from social expectations. Children, teens, and young adults should be encouraged to express themselves in positive and healthy ways, even when that expression doesn't reflect the gendered standards of past generations. As a high school librarian, I now see every day how students are becoming more capable of expressing themselves and challenging gendered expectations.

It is still very easy for me to fall into the old habit of repressing my feelings because I didn't learn how to express my own desires at a young age. Passivity was ingrained in many of my responses, but I do my best to counteract this pattern by respectfully expressing my current feelings to others. I no longer question the legitimacy of my emotions because I realize that I cannot control them. I can accept my desires for what they are—a part of living—and process them in healthy ways as they flow through me.

Processing these emotions means expressing them in relationships. As humans, we should feel comfortable communicating our feelings to one another. We are a social species. It is part of our survival to share our emotions with others. Emotions help us provide each other with crucial information about what we need to be healthy and happy. Even with negative emotions, acknowledging why we're upset helps us find solutions. Living, feeling, and sharing our desires opens the door for growth and companionship.

One of the things that I've learned about myself as I've started being more honest about my feelings is that sometimes I need time to know what I truly want. Often, I still need to untangle the various emotions and outside influences impacting me. But, listening to my feelings like this and recognizing when I need time has helped me navigate decisions. When you're navigating decisions for yourself, it is okay to tell people that you will get back to them with an answer. And, in sexual situations, when you're unsure, move slow. You should feel comfortable asking for space and time when you need it.

My husband and I now have a tendency to linger when it comes to sex. We will literally move slowly, asking how we feel along the way. We started doing this because I was not always sure of how I wanted to proceed when it came to our sexual interactions. I would think sex sounded nice, but then I would get afraid of it becoming painful again. We've now learned that if we move slowly and sensually, my body and I have time to figure out what I want, and if it isn't sex in that moment, it isn't the end of the world. We just stop or we choose to proceed with other forms of intimacy, which for us takes the form of naked spooning, kissing, or just simply talking to one another.

Reflection Questions

- Do you feel capable of expressing how you feel? Do you feel comfortable expressing how you feel?

- If so, how do you express yourself? In healthy or destructive ways? If not, what prevents you from expressing yourself?

- Do the people close to you support or criticize your self expression?

- Who are people in your life that make you feel safe expressing yourself?

- What are some healthy ways that you can express yourself to others?

Practice Action

Find or create a space for yourself. It doesn't have to be a private place. It can be a café, a library, an art studio, a hiking trail, or anywhere else where you feel comfortable. One of the things that has really helped me cope with my anxiety is finding spaces where I can take time for myself. For me, these spaces are very connected with being outside. Working in my small garden or going on a hike are some of the ways that I clear my mind. Often, an outdoor space is exactly what I need to get clarity on how to move forward when it comes to big decisions or just day-to-day interactions. Find a space for you to be you!

YOU CAN ALWAYS TALK TO ME

ADVENTURER:
Ebby, or, Through Pinocchio's Looking-Glass

Robert Thomas Greene

My father gave me a ride home the other day and awkwardly asked me what book he could buy me, since we're complete strangers to each other. Distant and tongue-tied, as I often was shortly after the scandal, I told him I'd been reading F. Scott Fitzgerald's short story collection that my buddy Jim from New York had lent me. Anyway, he did not seem too interested in my reverence for the works of this early twentieth century giant, so I adopted my glassy stare before arriving home to meet Mother for dinner.

·　　　·　　　·

"I opened the door and he stood there, fresh-skinned and glowing. There was something about his eyes….He had that starry-eyed look." (Alcoholics Anonymous, page 9).

·　　　·　　　·

Last summer, I walked into the seven a.m. meeting of Alcoholics Anonymous and sat down

at the back, sweaty from biking and holding my coffee.

There he was, a few rows in front of me, and something deep in my chest smiled the second I saw him.

He raised his hand as an available sponsor, and the rest of the meeting was entirely a blur—before I knew it I approached him, shyly and confidently all at once. Was he wearing a red baseball cap?

Reader, bear with me—let me take you back a few years. Before I moved to New York, I had a close friend I will call Ralph (a nod to Beverly Cleary). We would grab coffee every Tuesday before our meetings. He was a tall, white, Marine goofball and my teddy bear. We would joke about our respective sex addictions and bond over Selena Gomez. Sadly, we are now estranged, but I loved him very dearly and it was he whom I perceived in the man sitting a few rows ahead of me.

My inner child, whom I shall call Pinocchio, rebelled against reason and morality and got what he wanted. Ebby[1] shook my hand and gave me his

1 Ebby Thacher, an unsung hero, was the sponsor of Bill Wilson, a co-founder of Alcoholics Anonymous. I have taken the liberty to

phone number. We were to pray on it, as he was my newly-minted temporary sponsor.

He called within the week and asked me if I would prefer having a female sponsor because of my "sexuality." I felt myself get hot in the face and my throat strained. My fear of losing this potential connection and resentment at being immediately feminized flared all the way up.

"I'm not going to be sponsored by a woman." I was surprised at my tone and conviction.

"Alright. How's your relationship with God?"

"Stale."

At the AA breakfast, he introduced me to his wife, Trixie, who is about my age, and as beautiful as any wife of his would be. The two of them beamed at me, and my fantasy was born. Instantly, they became my favorite literary characters, Richard and Nicole Diver from F. Scott Fitzgerald's *Tender Is the Night:* the psychiatrist who married his patient and the darlings of the French Riviera. In my mind, I became the young actress Rosemary

use his name to protect anonymity and to introduce an archetype of the helping figure.

Hoyt, who adored the Divers and was Richard's mistress.

I needed him to be in my world and wanted him to love me, and so I rode the pink cloud[2] with full-blown ecstasy. Hosting a rooftop frittata dinner in the glitzy part of town, I invited him and Trixie, as well as his sponsor, co-sponsee, and his girlfriend to the place where I was house-sitting. I saluted this fantasy honeymoon with the new hero by my side. Another gentleman from my past sex life, Trey, also joined us, as deep down I wanted to see if Ebby and my AA people would accept me for my darkness. I made all of us wear blue so that I could see Ebby's eyes stand out against the stars. On the rooftop, I timidly approached him and smiled. *Jay Gatsby and Daisy Buchanan could not hold a candle to us.* In reality, he was slightly annoyed that I interrupted him and Trixie talking with the soft intensity of a married couple. When his mouth met hers, I snapped out of 1934. Denial shuddered through me; *No, surely I was not layering reality already.* Tearing my eyes away, I impulsively went and kissed Trey. Later that night, after everyone

2 A "pink cloud" in AA refers to a time during one's recovery that is rosy and short-lived by nature.

else left, Trey and I had vacant sex, after which Trey said, "Yeah, that Ebby guy, he's a stud."

"He's my sponsor," I proudly replied.

During the glorious beginning, Ebby, my late chihuahua-dachshund, and I would meet to do stepwork. My subterranean pyramid scheme waltzed along to the sanctity of his home. There was a photo of my dog and me in their living room I had given Ebby and Trixie to compel myself into their lives. Ebby told me about his past in the Marines and how he got sober, while I melted inside at the contrast of his blue shirt and green eyes against his pearly skin.

Trixie eventually became uncomfortable with having me over. She would fuss about the cleanliness of the home. I wanted more privacy with Ebby anyway, so we eventually met at a bookstore and then at a little idyllic park by my parents' house. I was experiencing, through artificial means, the family I never had. While we read the *Twelve Steps and the Twelve Traditions*, it became difficult for me to tell the difference between his devout Christian love and selflessness and my selfish love for him. We

developed the intimacy of a sponsor and sponsee while I continued to build my alternate reality.

Looking back now, my body was trying to warn me of impending trauma. Inexplicable grief overwhelmed me when he went on vacation for a few weeks. The perplexity came from a growing sense of unethical behavior on my part. Unfortunately, when he came back, I suppressed this awareness while we trudged along the Steps. There was nothing I wanted more than to be his earnest pupil and share an intellectual connection with him so that I could feel as masculine as he. Shocking and addicting was his camaraderie and spiritual nature; here's a cliché for you: I was a self-abandoning moth to a flame.

Preparing for the fifth step, which would require confessing the entirety of my wrongs to another human being, I was ready to impress him with my deepest insights about my past. Little did I know what was to come.

When I finally delivered the fifth step on October 23, 2021, my entire sense of self and peace of mind collapsed before me. I immediately dove into the intense vulnerability required to share my entire self with him, beginning with something extremely difficult to discuss. I shared a deeply held resentment for my sister for calling me a fag in front of her boyfriend when I was eighteen or nineteen, before I was open about my sexuality. There was a breathless pause as I waited for his comfort. His response was to point out how it was common among him and his brothers growing up, that it was not a big deal, especially if my sister did not know that I'm gay.

A stunned silence followed as the image I didn't know I had made of him faded. I felt small, stupid, and self-conscious unto this strange man. Yes, I knew he was right about forgiving my sister, but in a flash I had lost the fatherly sponsor I had invented; the one who would tell me, "I get it man. I love you." I gathered my glasses and papers and wanted to run, run, run!

Ebby asked for forgiveness, while doubling down, and warned me against "putting him on a pedestal." With unbearable shock, it dawned on me: I had filled in the blanks of a man I barely knew and sought the wrong person for understanding and compassion. My willful denial of the cultural differences between us burned to the ground. I felt the real him materialize next to me, and for a fleeting moment, a real person sat next to him as well.

At a further point in my fifth step, I blurted out my romantic feelings for him. He shut his eyes for a few seconds and said, "Okay." After six hours of revealing a lifelong chain of lies, I said, "Here lies strewn my house of cards," to which he responded, "It's time to rebuild a real one." After we hugged and he walked away, I turned back to look at him as if for the last time.

The Big Book of AA recommends a period of solitude and reflection after sharing a fifth step. When I got home, however, I realized the world I had created for survival had just ended. I threw myself at my roommate's feet and sobbed, "I told him everything!" A horrifying awareness of what I had done, that I had defrauded myself from the start, prevented me from having any sense of peace for weeks to come. I repeatedly sought his reassurance that he wouldn't leave me after what I shared, with a gnawing, torturous feeling that it was I who needed to leave the relationship.

The intense intimacy I had shared with him in telling him all of my deepest secrets had backfired on me, and I developed Posttraumatic Stress Disorder. For several months, sleep was impossible, and I was accosted by nightmares that medication could barely mitigate. With unflinching force, my heart would gnaw at me to leave Ebby. I would fight it, emailing Brosef (as we'd call each other) nightly inventories and spiritual poems in profuse obsession and denial.

Words like fraud, impostor, and whore were my mates and meals. I would pace the house back and forth and confess more and more to my mother before speeding off to an AA meeting, where I was a shadowy glob in sweats and a hoodie sitting in the back, rocking back and forth. Obsession with Ebby and obsession with denying my obsession dominated me. Rationalizations such as *"Ebby. I… I love you spiritually…right? Right?! We can finish the twelve steps"* would sear through my brain.

Even though Ebby knew the truth and had forgiven me, my heart insisted that I take drastic action to save my life and prevent further harm. It was alarmingly clear to me that I was sacrificing my integrity and recovery for the sake of keeping him in my life. Attempting to work the sixth and seventh steps, which require fundamental change, became an absolute disaster. Most tellingly, I was entangled in grieving my loss of humanity and barely functioning during a time that I was supposed to be repairing my life and relationships. As a result, the amends I squeezed out to my sister was hollow and forced, since I was not sober.

Stubbornly, however, I fed the monster of denial, getting high on every one of Ebby's words and loving texts. Guilt and shame colored my sexual obsession with him and his fraternity while I continued to fabricate a nonexistent bromance. Being around him was becoming no different than snorting cocaine. Rapidly, I lost the ability to attend to my basic needs, such as eating and sleeping. The worst of my horror and shame happened after his explanation of humility. His bravado-filled warning against "walking into an AA meeting pumping our cocks" with the accompanying hand gestures was too much for me to bear. Violent nightmares and panic attacks would not let me forget the lie I was sustaining to myself. The time had come for me to be honest with myself, this hollow wooden-puppet

I had become. In December 2021, I emailed Ebby goodbye, thanking him for all he had done, and asked him to cease contact.

• • •

Although our relationship was real, it had stopped being healthy. I had created an alternate world where Ebby was my father, protector, friend, God, and brother at the expense of developing a relationship with myself. Coming to accept that I had lost myself in a man who was there to help me lead a healthier life initially brought gnawing pangs of burning regret. The reflection in the mirror was ghostly, and I felt as if Pinocchio's assertion had clusterfucked itself into a question. "Am I a real man?" It took months to rebuild a sense of humanity.

Ebby and I have never spoken again, and it has taken all year to discover who I really am without toxic dependence on him. Those first few months without him were pure agony, but I know that seeking him out would undermine the reconstructive process that writing and solitude have provided me. Rethinking the regret of losing Ebby, I am grateful for learning the value

of authenticity and for realizing how little I have cultivated my own sense of manhood. From the first time Ebby said, "I love you, brother," I was startled when he saw something in me that he saw in himself. An ocean of disbelief and joy swelled inside me when he called me his bro. Being his bro had become the perfect way to distract myself from the lack of fulfillment or interest I feel around gay men.

I thought I had it all figured out. In my alternate universe, he would never break my heart because we could never actually be together, so we would therefore eternally maintain a platonic, intimate relationship. Reality showed me, however, the consequences of inventing the dad I desperately needed as a child and young man. I saw in Ebby the muscular son-in-law who would protect me from my abusive father and be the object of my mother's doting. I wanted my parents' approval of him to fill the space their rejection left. Frankenstein's monster- was really myself, the beloved son masquerading as a pseudo-sober sponsee. When would it stop?

Let me tell you about my ex-husband-to-be: a skincare professional in Los Angeles. Our sudden break-up in 2017 set me up for my preference for multilayered platonic relationships with heterosexual men. He was more than twice my age, and I felt on top of the world, believing I was free from my abusive past and promised a life of excitement and love. I repressed my ongoing discomfort at being his mannequin, and it threw Leslie off when I would call him *Daddy* nonconsensually. Compulsively, I would superimpose the imaginary alpha male to avoid loving and being loved by the real one. My error suffocated the space where we could intimately be ourselves and resolve conflict.

Sudden exposure to his verbal abuse and his suffering from my disorganized nature and untreated depression ended our engagement. I have never had a boyfriend since. Since then, I unconsciously started seeking emotional intimacy with heterosexual men, afraid of experiencing once more the trauma of sudden loss. It felt safer for straight men to love me and gay men to fuck me—fantasy would build the bridge! Through a choreography of mental gymnastics, I could be close to men without running the risk of losing them if I never really had them. The resulting loneliness now prevents me from trying to control the universe through self-dishonesty and creating impossibly entangled scenarios. Up until Ebby, however, I had never gone so far as to compromise my basic sense of self to such horrifying lengths.

For the majority of my adulthood, I sought escape from emptiness through my relationships. Jarringly, my father's response to my former engagement—a question, "Do you expect me to applaud you?"—unconsciously pushed me to seek the support and validation of straight men who celebrated me where he never did. With Ebby's love, I was doomed from the start, obsessed with finding ways to be there for him emotionally. Disentangling myself from him and his memory, I have learned that nothing is worth living dishonestly.

To avoid confronting the sabotage and failure of my relationship with Leslie, I had tried to recreate him, to some degree, in Ralph. When that friendship ended, I tried finding Ralph in Ebby. Rather than accept loneliness, I behaved as a naive puppy or a little boy looking for his stuffed animal. As much as I am accused of being an idealist, I have known what it was like to be in a mutually romantic relationship without altering reality. Leslie had the original kindness I perceived from Ebby and about which I once wrote so many poems. What survives is the connection I found to the godliness in all living things. Having now internally said goodbye to Leslie helps me understand how to love other men without losing myself in the hopes that they could resemble him *or reassemble me.*

There are lessons about consent in this narrative. Without his consent, I had turned Ebby into my Higher Power. Without my own consent, I launched my own ethical code into the cosmos and traded my authenticity for belonging and protection. Ultimately, the core boundary violation I committed was between reality and unreality: I created a false self who was satisfied with a mutation of intimacy. In seeking to be close to Ebby through engineered means, I dissociated from myself. I have learned a healthy boundary keep my fantasy-driven and kinky nature from causing psychological harm.

I have always needed fraternal belonging *while bringing my true self to the table.* Direct, transparen

relationships are more satisfying than having someone as a surrogate dad. Although I will always have my Achilles heel, psychological integrity and the absence of shame are sexier than sacrificing myself. Excitedly, I have found a leather bar to be a safer space to explore my submissive kink, and have found BDSM to produce healing experiences from last year's horror. I even want to explore pup play!

Thankfully, I have men in my life now who *do* get it; who *do* provide and receive emotional support without me having to sign my soul over to the devil. My ex-sponsor was someone who tried to help me, but got a facsimile. The real me would have remembered Leslie and Ralph that fateful morning and pedaled furiously away. The real me would have known Ebby was rather aloof. Importantly, I've learned to chill out when it comes to masculinity.

And now, do join me, Reader, in cremating the former wooden image of my inner child.

Pinocchio's ashes spread across the psych meds and ebbing nightmares as trauma goes astray.

If there is anything that persists from the person I was during this haunting period of my life, it is the forgiveness and love I experienced from Ebby's sponsor, Will. During my erratic days between October and December 2021, I fled to NYC and confessed everything to him over the phone, sobbing from Jim's kitchen floor in Richmond Hill. He did not judge me nor did he banish me as his grandsponsee. He saw the person behind the partition and forgave me. His last words to me were, "I look forward to seeing you at the seven a.m. meeting on Saturday." Will planted the hope to someday demonstrate this level of humanity towards a person in need. Alas, I only ask to become like the real Ebby Thacher, free from bootlegged identities. Glory be to helping a student with their writing, cooking chili, or raising a glass to the end of the Prohibition Era, sharing with you that starry-eyed look.

•   •   •

"Keep on walking on this road, where you become more human and more divine." (from *The Gospel of Mary Magdalene*).

CHAPTER 3: TACKLING GENDER ROLES

Resentment Towards Men

When I realized that many of my negative patterns were a result of my socialization within emotional gender roles, I felt frustrated. I was deeply disturbed by the privilege that many men held in personal relationships. I had to understand who I was outside of all of the regret, but I initially couldn't see past the anger. Resentment towards men and "masculine" personalities brewed within me even before I recognized the fallacy of gender roles. I always felt like societal ideas of strength were unfair and biased, but as I started recognizing these inequalities in my own relationships, my anger expanded into resentment.

Traditional expectations placed on women in relationships contributed to my resentment towards men. I always knew that I didn't want to change my name if I ever got married, I knew that I didn't feel very nurturing towards children, and I knew that I was no longer going to stifle my own sexual desires. In many ways, my resentment was fueled by envy that men could have all of the same preferences as me without being judged for

them. But, more than any perceived judgment, my resentment towards men came from observations and experiences regarding sex with men. I had the impression that most men objectified women when it came to sex, and I was incredibly frustrated by what felt like my inevitable future as someone sexually attracted primarily to men.

Resentment became an inevitable part of my relationships as issues went unresolved and power inequalities remained intact. Saying "sorry" a million times and holding in my feelings had resulted in an overabundance of internal anger and frustration. My thoughts and emotions had often trailed behind me even after I realized that I had the ability to take control of my life. These emotional remnants from the past would throw tantrums like little children instead of allowing me to express my maturity. They were the anxiety and resentment that I was taught to have in matters of men. But they did not stem from feminism. They stemmed from being taught that men would judge me for my body, that men would not like me if I was too assertive about my sexuality, and that men would disrespect me if I "gave it up" too quickly. They came from being taught that I would need a man to take care of me, a man to be "the man" in the relationship, a man who would outwardly control me.

These feelings came from living in a patriarchal society where men, good or bad, have been viewed as more powerful than women. I learned from many outlets—family, news, movies— that women should be protected by men and that if "good men" weren't around, I could be attacked by the "bad ones." Women should not feel the need to carry pepper spray or wield their keys as weapons when they are out and alone at night, but stories of rape and assault leave every woman on guard. Any time I had to walk home in the dark by myself, I would end up running because I was afraid. Any time I had plans to travel alone, I would instead invite someone out of what I thought was necessity. Any time a boy showed interest in me, I thought I had to play hard to get if I wanted him to respect me. I had been trained to blindly believe the power that men could have over me.

The inhibitions that I learned in childhood continued to challenge my personal wants and needs. I was wary of becoming too involved

with men. I believed that only desperate women put themselves in danger by expressing their sexual desire. I was taught to distrust nearly half of humanity, and as a result, I learned to distrust my own feelings about that humanity. Instead of trusting myself, I played into the roles that the patriarchy had cast for me. Male authority figures, even my own male partners, felt like a threat to me. The power they had within our culture made it easy to blame individual men for societal problems. Despite knowing well-intentioned men who aren't brutish and disrespectful, my anxiety and resentment held me back from communicating with them.

On the other hand, despite being an intelligent person who generally knows what I want in this world, I always felt insecure when my gender preferences that fell outside of heterosexual norms were questioned. Whether it was who I wanted to be with or how I wanted to be with them, many people showed concern for my desires that fell outside of their idea of a straight female. One close family member cried over my interest in a woman. Others told me that the reason I had relationship problems was because I wasn't dating manly enough men. All of these people thought they were helping me, but each disapproval was a reminder of the judgment I would receive if I didn't follow the rules of heterosexual dating, creating another kind of resentment altogether.

Learning To Be Myself

While it wasn't easy, looking back on the dysfunction in my past relationships and embracing new experiences taught me how to be myself, rather than harbor resentments in relationships. The dysfunctional couple is so common that we can all immediately understand what that looks like and means. I've lived it, and it is all too likely that you have as well. Friends and family witnessed me closing myself off in relationships.

In each new relationship, it quickly became my priority to keep "the honeymoon phase" intact. I thought apologizing incessantly or keeping resentment inside would help; however, all it did was postpone the conflict and prevent me from expressing myself. Once the resentment built up to the point of bursting, even forming sentences to

describe my emotions felt like an insurmountable feat. When I inevitably became depressed about the relationship, I couldn't process my emotions internally, let alone explain them to someone else. It felt like it was too late. It felt like no one could understand me, so I resorted to silence.

When I would get stuck in believing that no one understood me, it was easy to fall back on gender stereotypes. Guys were dicks. Girls were bitches. The "us against them" mentality infiltrated my depression, and "them" could be men or women at polarized ends of the gender spectrum. I found it difficult to love without resentment, particularly in sexual relationships. In my mind, everyone became the girly girl or the manly man. I couldn't see past my own judgments to develop relationships with others. When I had extreme negative emotions, I cut ties and pushed people away. I saw no way to repair the resentment, anger, and sadness. I would try to replace relationships, but I did not know how to repair my view of people.

Among my classmates in college, I saw how there was a negative connotation associated with women's studies, so I purposely avoided courses on gender as long as I could. I didn't want to be the person in class who always pointed out, "What about the women?" I thought I could ignore the power dynamics in relation to gender and emotions, but I was only harming myself. I needed to explore alternative environments where people had different views of gender in order to begin forming healthy relationships. I needed to understand that there is always an alternative way to view and live one's life.

Thankfully I had to take a course on gender to fulfill a requirement for my major, but I only took the course because it was required, and once again it was only accessible in a privileged place. After the course, I finally began to understand the possibilities of gender in regards to myself and others. I learned how people can express gender in different ways, and I began to understand the possibilities for my own relationships. I realized how important it was to find a new understanding of the world so that my love could be healthy, supportive, and balanced.

I started exploring my own gender and I eventually accepted that I am nonbinary, meaning

that I don't identify as a woman or a man. I still haven't changed pronouns in my day-to-day life because I've only told my husband and a few close friends and family members (and my current counselor of course!). Thankfully, at this point, everyone has been supportive, but more importantly, accepting my gender identity has helped me recognize my own identity and self-worth outside of other people's thoughts and opinions. I think eventually I will be more open about being nonbinary, but I'm taking my time and moving at a pace that works well for me.

I used to think that social norms always caused more suffering for women than men; however, it became clear over time that gender norms hurt all people by limiting acceptable identities and forms of expression. Whether we have white privilege, straight privilege, or any other trait that society arbitrarily elevates, we can examine how our privilege hurts others and live our lives in a way that attempts to reduce suffering. People of every gender imaginable are forced to struggle with societal expectations. In small and large ways, strict ideas of masculinity in particular can jeopardize equality for all of us.

Struggling with Masculinity

One of the men I dated for a short period of time brought to my attention how men also struggle with gender norms in relationships. Although this man was liberal and theoretically supportive of feminism, he constantly tried to become "the provider" in our relationship. He believed that the failure of his last relationship was due to his inability to support his ex-girlfriend. He felt disappointed in himself anytime I paid for a meal. Though I told him I was happy to pay for our dates, his self-esteem suffered because he could never fulfill his expectations of masculinity. He felt that he had to reach a certain level of financial security to be a successful man. By doing so, he abandoned his individual talents as an artist and writer to pursue the more "manly" venture of computer science. We did not continue our relationship for long, so I cannot testify to his happiness now, but I can tell you that he seemed unhappy and did not do well in the computer science classes that he clearly had no real interest in. It is not surprising, however, that he attempted to go down that path, as our society disproportionately rewards male-dominated career

choices to the detriment of those who choose an alternative path.

Another male friend of mine suffered deeply in his relationships due to societal views of men and sexuality. Raised in a household with traditional Judeo-Christian views of sexual orientation, he suppressed his feelings for other men. Though his female partner accepted his attraction to men, he continually struggled and failed to understand his own sexuality. He couldn't reconcile his identity as a man with his bisexuality. He knew others who challenged traditional notions of male sexuality, but his upbringing barred him from accepting his own. The societal criticism and judgment of bisexual men was enough to keep him from being open about his own feelings.

After I graduated college, I continued taking community college classes, which in many ways turned out to be much more educational than my university courses. In one of the gender studies courses that I had signed up for, a transgender man who worked with our local LGBTQ center came to a class to tell us about his experiences. He detailed how he had seen the world from both sides of the traditional gender binary. He experienced being called stupid and dependent by his ex-husband when he was female bodied. And then, despite liking kids, and having grandchildren himself, he experienced mothers steering their children away from him because he was a middle-aged man. He saw how his life was restricted in different ways on both sides of the gender divide but also recognized that he generally experienced more privilege as a man in social interactions.

It took years for him to realize that if he wasn't being himself, he would be severely depressed. Before he started talking about his struggles and living as himself, he had attempted suicide multiple times. Unfortunately, this kind of experience is not uncommon for transgender people. A 2015 survey by the UCLA Williams Institute found that 46 percent of transgender people surveyed had experienced verbal harassment and 9 percent had experienced physical violence in the prior year as a result of being targeted for their gender identity. Combining the rates of violence against transgender people with the disproportionate suicide risk, it is painfully clear that societal views of gender are taking lives.

The men described above suffered to varying degrees because of their traits that didn't fit with gender norms. At some point in their lives, they realized that it was degrading for someone who is perceived as a man to take on "feminine" roles. To combat negative beliefs towards women and anyone who is perceived as "feminine," it is necessary for all men to express how patriarchy affects their lives.

The journey towards respect for oneself is a long one. We're socialized to be concerned about how people view us rather than to take the initiative to learn about how others prefer to be, but as things gradually change, we can learn to shift our focus from internal regrets and resentments to respect for ourselves and others.

CONSIDER THIS

Reflection Questions

- In your relationships, do you have specific expectations of your partner(s) based on their gender? Example: Expecting men to pay for dates in heterosexual relationships.

- Do you ever find yourself associating negative traits with other genders? If so, then where do you think those perceptions come from?

- Have you ever felt resentment towards a partner? What was the source of the resentment? Did it relate to any perceived gender expectations?

Practice Action

If you are cisgender, meaning that you identify as the same gender assigned to you at birth, try something, anything, that stretches your gender norms. This will mean different things for different people since we don't all adhere to the same view of gender. This could mean shopping in a different gender's clothing department or experimenting with various shaving and grooming habits. Try something that you wouldn't usually do out of fear of judgment because of your gender. See how it feels. Maybe you won't like it and that's okay, but maybe you'll love it!

If you're nonbinary or transgender, you've likely felt forced to act as another gender throughout your life due to societal expectations, so you should skip this one, just simply be proud of yourself for being you!

Schrödinger's Dick: It's Yours, It's Beautiful, and It's Enough

Duc Tran

"It is a peculiar sensation, this double-consciousness, this sense of always looking at one's self through the eyes of others."   —W.E.B. Du Bois

I hate to do this to my idol, W.E.B. Du Bois, but I realized in the years around 9/11 that I had Double Dick Consciousness. It was like experiencing Schrödinger's cat on a penile level. The theory from quantum physics works like this: while the cat is inside the box with a substance that can kill it, it is both alive *and* dead until we open the box. It inhabits both poles of a binary state while the box is closed. Having an Asian dick also meant belonging to two entirely different conceptions: an Asian dick was both insatiable and inadequate; it procreated but didn't fuck; it wasn't big enough to be worth a conversation, but its smallness *was* the conversation. It was everything and it was nothing.

Had I been more aware of this double consciousness, I believe I could have been a better person, a better man in my late teens and twenties

But I don't think a lot of Asian men collectively had the language to convey to each other and to others how this felt. Instead, we muddled about, drifting from one toxic model of masculinity to another.

The defining moment didn't happen in a wee wooden schoolhouse in New England; rather, it happened as a bunch of Asian-American boys and I ogled chesty models in *Maxim* magazine in a high school weight room reeking of Axe deodorant and desperation.

I don't remember the issue cover, but there was an article on global penis sizes. All of us assumed there was nothing wrong with our metrics, until we saw the list: Asian guys were dead last in this study. There was a silence in the weight room as we all tried to absorb this news: *now what*?

It all came to us at once: it was the prime mover behind Jet Li's flaccid side hug with Aaliyah in *Romeo Must Die* despite risking his life for ninety minutes trying to save her, the reason why our older brothers and cousins were called "Donger" in high school in the eighties, the root of our obsession with Black masculinity throughout the nineties, the explanatory note for why we fetishized white girls as we exclusively dated Asian ones. It explained why so many of our peers leaned into the whole "Pickup Artist" thing in the early aughts that reduced women to a series of affinities and tendencies like monsters in a *Final Fantasy* bestiary. We collectively said it in our own heads at the same time, the way Jerry says, "Newman!" on *Seinfeld*: "Asian dick!"

It was karmic in a way. Many root cultures of Asia had their own problems with women's oppression, from the practice of sati to the Three Obediences toward father, husband, and eldest son. Maybe we deserved it, and the Western lens on masculinity was our just reward.

At the same time, the early 2000s was a weird time for masculinity in America, but frankly it's always a weird time for masculinity in America. Fox News had 24-hour footage of heroic young men rolling through the desert towards Baghdad as the less heroic were buying *Girls Gone Wild* DVDs and reading Tucker Max blog entries on the good old Web 2.0 back home. Paris Hilton and Kim Kardashian launched the sextape arms race and launched an equally weird time for feminism

as the line blurred between women's sexual agency and exploitation.

Most of the Western literary canon belongs in a section called "White Man Fears Death, Hilarity Ensues." Sex and death have gone together (viz: the *femme fatale* tropes in film noir, the entirety of Greek mythology, at least three-quarters of Shakespeare, and all of Hemingway, Mailer, and Roth), but after 9/11 the subtext became the text.

We were blowing up people in sandy places with unpronounceable names while at home we obsessed over who was blowing whom. I point this out because growing up in America, the white lens on the world was the standard for understanding yourself. Asian men understood ourselves not on our own terms, but in the way white people saw us, constantly trying to live up to their expectations, but at the same time impotently trying to defy them. And realizing our identity was defined by the stereotype of an inadequate penis, well, fucked us up. It was like an STD; if you talked about it, it must mean it was true about you.

It's odd to think that somehow Asian-Americans were unwillingly roped into this national mass hysteria of a death-and-sex cult. Back then, there was a website called gayorasian.com that asked people to pick whether an Asian dude was gay, or just, y'know, Asian. *The Daily Show*, a liberal safe space that specialized in get-a-load-of-this-guy segments mocking the neoconservative agenda, aired a piece on an Asian-American professor seeking to make Asian men more visible in adult films. The producers clearly had a good snicker at the guy, but I couldn't help but wish him some success.

In college, my professor during our general history course offered us extra credit if we read and wrote about a pornographic novel from the Ming dynasty called *The Carnal Prayer Mat*, wherein the main character grafted his penis with a dog's to increase its size. No context or reason was given; we could have read other classics from the same period like *Water Margin*, or *Journey to the West*. But no, we had to read the dick-enlarging novel. A good friend of mine, a white woman, told me to my face I must have a small penis because I was Asian the same way someone might point out a

I heard girls in my Asian social group actively talk about wanting to date white guys with the same level of reverse exoticism. My friend in college wrote on her Xanga blog exclusively about how much she hated Asian men (update: she's happily married to one and has two kids with him). She hated their awkwardness, their self-segregation. She hated their nerdiness, their inability to be "just one of the guys" who drank domestic beer and talked a little too loudly about their fantasy football teams. She basically hated them for not being white enough.

In my family, one of our aunts divorced her husband from Vietnam and dated a white man. During the family get-togethers she was like a prophet to the other women, a Jeremiah in polyester and suede pumps: "White men treat us like queens, while Viet men expect us to treat them like kings! You should see the kinds of things Rick would do for me."

And I wonder now if we were, collectively, Asian men and women, having a moment in which we needed to have a dialogue with ourselves, amongst ourselves, but somehow the only way to do this was through the mediating lens of whiteness and otherness. The thing was, maybe some of the women above had a point. A lot of our dads kind of forgot how to be husbands, fathers, in a connected way that white dads so easily did. Their emotional disconnection and emphasis on sweating endlessly at jobs they hated for their kids really did emotionally neuter their children as they grew up watching white families on TV have difficult but honest conversations.

And as for straight Asian men, we were kind of adrift in a nebulous space. As children we were little princelings in the household, but outside many of us struggled to fit in in non-Asian spaces. We weren't exotic; we were just foreign.

We watched shitty programming like *The Man Show*, fantasizing that maybe one day Adam Carolla or Joe Rogan would want to hang out with us. We tried white people things like camping and playing indie rock covers on guitar, and spiking our hair like those guys from *Jersey Shore*. My cousin changed his name to Martin, joined a rock climbing gym, and bagged himself a white girl who both had relatives in the Midwest who couldn't dance

and could still eat fermented shrimp paste. He's still the gold standard in my family to this day.

I know it's not original to talk about Asian-American self-hate, but it cannot be understated how many Asian men hated ourselves then, and perhaps still. And it was a specific form of racism that tied itself to America's anxiety about its own virility, its own power in the context of its imperial impulses.

After 9/11 America wanted to fuck shit up, but it needed foils to keep up the mission. On the one hand, it had the racist caricature of the freedom-hating hajji in the Middle East, who was both insidiously threatening and comically backward, medieval in morality, but adaptively cunning. At home, those who unironically said "freedom fries" saw themselves beset by shrill feminists and beta males who tried to get in the way of the fun. The Dixie Chicks got canceled before "canceling" was a thing for speaking out against the Iraq war.

Asian men, long the targets of Western sexual anxieties, were easy because they have the eternal stink of "foreigner" on them. And in the days of Yellow Peril, if an Asian man married a white woman, she had to give up her US citizenship after the passing of the Expatriation Act of 1907. Asian dick apparently couldn't do much sexually, but it could wipe out birthright citizenship.

This is why the Schrödinger's cat motif kept coming up for me. America couldn't pick a lane when it comes to why it hated and belittled us: Asian men were both ineffectual and menacing at the same time. At least in the old-timey binary world of Orientalism, "the East" consistently represented superstition and ignorance, while "the West" was enlightened and rational. It was racist, but at least consistent.

Even today, in our post-*Crazy Rich Asians*, "Stop Asian Hate" world of representation, there can still be more complex representations of Asian men. Don't get me wrong, guys like Steven Yeun, Henry Golding, and Simu Liu are way better to look up to than what I had growing up. All we had were the ghost of Bruce Lee, Bruce Li, Bruce Lai, and dubbed versions of Jackie Chan. But at the same time, even when I see Asian men represented as objects of desire in Hollywood, they are not often

in and of themselves desirable. They still seem, to be frank, still rather sexless.

In film noir, there is the concept of a "dame with a rod," a woman who has something extra (a gun, a working vagina, a brain) who jars the power imbalance in the moral world of the movie. This is why these films were only menacing if you're a white man. If you see women as human beings, it's a satisfying revenge flick.

Whether it's Nick Young from *Crazy Rich Asians*, or Glenn from *The Walking Dead*, all these dudes were just "dames with a rod." What made Nick desirable was his wealth and access to power, even as he played the role of a pauper teaching economics in New York. Asian superheroes represented by Asian men weren't that different from Bruce Lee: they kicked ass but were always supernatural, not grounded in reality, in flesh and bone. They weren't in and of themselves desirable.

Maybe, though, the problem is just in our heads. Maybe I need to just get over my double-dick consciousness and just appreciate it. It does its job, and rather well. It's served my partner and me just fine, and most times better than fine. Maybe t's time for me to stop, in the words of Du Bois, "always looking at one's self through the eyes of others, of measuring one's soul by the tape of world that looks on in amused contempt and pity." It's probably time to put away the tape measure, the bitterness over these weak attempts at AAPI representation. Yes, we can be manly men on our own terms, whatever it means, without some Hollywood star to represent us.

And as the American empire winds down after our pullbacks from Iraq and Afghanistan, the impulse to define masculinity as rigidly aggressive and antagonistic today is just seen as corny by most people. The men today who promote that tough-guy posturing from post-9/11 are basically incel weirdos like Ben Shapiro and Josh Hawley. And, in a way, that's as satisfying an ending as I, an Asian-American man, could hope for. Maybe younger people and their appreciation for fluidity, gentleness as strength, an eye for aesthetics could shake up and redefine more descriptive ways of "being a man," whatever that means. If I could speak to my younger self back then, I'd let him know: "Love yourself, love your dick. It's yours, it's

STEREOTYPICAL GENDER SPECTRUM

FEMALE

MAKEUP

EMOTIONAL

GROOMING

SPORTS

AGGRESSION

MALE

CHAPTER 4:
ESTABLISHING
BOUNDARIES

Why Boundaries Are Important

Figuratively speaking, there are two ways of pushing boundaries. One way is healthy, the other destructive. Sometimes we think of pushing our own boundaries as a way of overcoming fears. After processing all of the regret and resentment that I had felt in my teens and twenties, I knew that I was ready for a new beginning. In moments of growth, it's natural to want to try new things, and we may discover that changing our own boundaries results in positive change.

On the other hand, the negative form of pushing boundaries means causing emotional damage by disregarding another person's boundaries. The individual may be a lover, a friend, or a stranger. The act may be physical, sexual, emotional, or all of the above. Whether intentional or unintentional, if you've crossed someone else's boundaries, you've hurt them. You can cross divides in great ways when you are empowered and respecting the limits of those around you. But you should not use your own sexual or social liberation to pressure

another person into a compromising situation. It's important to recognize the distinction.

We all know that person who can't take no for an answer. Even in small day-to-day interactions, there are people who will push their thoughts and opinions on other people. Maybe you have even been that person! Think about times when you have felt adamantly that you knew what was best and right, even when someone was telling you that whatever you were pushing wasn't right for them. Be aware if you have the tendency to think you know what is "best" or "normal" or "right," and reflect on how you responded to others in those situations. You always have the right to develop and change. Cross all the boundaries you want as long as you recognize that you cannot force others to join you. If you use your personal choices or preferences to justify crossing someone else's boundaries, you will risk hurting another person, which is far from the goal of this journey.

Boundaries and Abuse

Examine your boundaries to see if they are compatible with the people around you. All relationships and people are different. A boundary may develop during a new experience or reappear from an old trauma. Disagreements in boundaries are expected when you interact with other people, yet the results of arguments vary greatly depending on people's maturity, respect, and support. When arguments escalate to ignoring a person's boundaries, however, the situation becomes abuse, and in more severe situations ignoring a person's boundaries can even become a physically violent act. All abusive interactions have one commonality—they all involve violating boundaries.

When it comes to different forms of abuse, physical abuse is generally easy for people to recognize and define. When a person intentionally hits another person, it is clear to us that the relationship is abusive. The obvious intent to harm another person through physical violence is clearly a problem to most people. But physical abuse can extend beyond obvious violence that leaves bruises. It should be equally as obvious to us that physical abuse is occuring when we talk about sexual assault and/or sexual coercion in

relationships. When a person is forcing someone to do anything physically, no matter the means, we should recognize that they are crossing universal boundaries by inflicting a form of physical violence on their partner(s).

While it may not be as clear, however, verbal interactions on their own, such as criticizing a person in a moment of anger, can also cause a great amount of emotional damage. Sometimes in our frustration, our own bias gets in our way and we think it's warranted. But there should be no doubt that when a person attacks a partner's insecurities, they are intentionally hurting them. We've all been there when we say something that we know will hurt someone else because we are mad or frustrated. Be aware if this is a pattern for you. Tell your partner that you need a moment to process things and walk away if you need to. When we're mad, we can feel like verbal harm is justified, but it's not. Insecurities should never be used as a weapon.

Personal boundaries can be unique to a specific person or relationship. Since we are all different people, things that bother me may not bother you and vice versa. This is why describing personal triggers to a partner is important to avoid unintentional harm. For instance, when I started dating my husband, I made it very clear that certain sexual positions and some types of dirty talk trigger negative emotional responses for me. I am aware that I have specific limits when it comes to sex due to my past experiences, but the only way he could know these things was through us communicating.

You may not be aware of all of your and your partner(s)' emotional triggers, and that's okay. I'm not saying you have to dive into your entire emotional history before every sexual interaction with another person. Just don't assume that you know all of your sexual partner(s)' boundaries. The important thing is to explore together at a pace that all participants are comfortable with. In cases where you are developing a long term sexual relationship, ensure that communication is continually open and evolving. Let the person know that you understand, that you are there for them, and that you also have your own personal boundaries. Communicate your own boundaries,

and when they're ready, ask your partner if they feel comfortable sharing their boundaries with you. "Are you comfortable with [fill in the blank]?" should be a common question in your relationships.

Your partner(s) may not be able to clearly explain their discomfort to you. You do not need to know what caused their boundaries to form. But you should pay attention to their body language and other attempts to create distance in case the person you're with is unable to clearly define or explain their boundaries. Many of us aren't raised to clearly express ourselves in uncomfortable situations. People exhibit a whole myriad of emotional responses to discomfort: some people freeze, some people cover things up with a joke, some people run. Get to know your partner(s) and gently ask questions if you notice some discomfort on their side so that you can better understand when they are uncomfortable with a sexual situation.

You don't need to know exactly why a partner is uncomfortable with something. They may not even know the reason themselves. It takes time to understand where emotional triggers come from.

They may not feel comfortable going into all of the details initially. Likewise, you may not want to share everything right away. While it can help you understand a person better to know why they have specific boundaries, ultimately it is not necessary for creating consent. You can respect a person's sexual boundaries without knowing the source of those boundaries.

Because emotional triggers can cause distrust and resentment, respecting each other's boundaries is crucial for the survival of any healthy relationship. Whether the damage seems big or small, denying someone's boundaries means denying them control over their own life. There will always be differences in how we perceive relationships, which is why conflict often occurs in intimate interactions. Discussing the conflict and respecting each other's boundaries can prevent a relationship from becoming fraught with unhealthy habits. Crossing another person's boundaries weakens trust within the relationship, and if you continually break someone's trust, they will only build more and more resentment towards you.

Ensure that you are paying attention to what you and your partner need to have a healthy sex life, and if you discover that you aren't compatible sexually, it is always okay to accept that someone isn't the right sexual partner for you. You and your partner(s) should never feel pressured to conform to each other's ideals for sex in an effort to "save" the relationship. If you aren't willing to respect a partner's boundaries or vice versa, it is time to consider other options, such as going to counseling, ending the relationship, exploring open relationships, or all of the above, before the relationship becomes abusive. You have the right to desire a certain kind of sex, love, and partnership, but you don't have a right to hurt others by forcing them to conform to your ideals.

If you are currently in an abusive relationship or if you have inflicted abuse on someone else, don't be afraid to reach out to someone you trust or call the National Domestic Violence Hotline to discuss your situation. Maybe you're not sure if what you're experiencing is abuse. That's okay! The volunteers at the National Domestic Violence Hotline are trained to help you understand your concerns about possible abuse in your relationships.

National Domestic Violence Hotline

Support and resources are available to people who have experienced abuse, as well as people who have perpetrated abuse and are looking to change, 24 hours, 7 days a week, 365 days a year in a variety of languages.

1-800-799-SAFE (7233) / thehotline.org

Maintaining Boundaries

Now that we've covered why boundaries are important and how the violation of boundaries can escalate into abuse, let's address the issue of maintaining sexual boundaries. While establishing and sharing your sexual boundaries with a partner can be difficult, maintaining boundaries is even harder. Just like any good habit, the hard part is following through. It is very important to note that the following advice is only meant for relationships that have not escalated into abusive situations. Abuse makes sexual situations dysfunctional at best and physically dangerous at worst. Reach out to a professional or someone else that you trust if you are concerned that you are in an abusive relationship.

When it comes to healthy sexual relationships, your job has two parts: (1) Checking in with yourself to ensure that you aren't denying or ignoring your own feelings when a partner makes you uncomfortable and (2) checking in with your partner(s) to ensure that you aren't making them feel uncomfortable. When I say check in, I'm not saying you have to do anything formal or official. All you need to do is pay attention. If you are uncomfortable with a sexual situation, communicate your concerns to your partner(s). If the boundary is related to a past trauma that you aren't ready to talk about yet, just remember that you don't need to explain why you have a boundary, you just need to let your partner(s) know that you are uncomfortable. If you are in a healthy relationship, your partner(s) will respect all of your sexual boundaries regardless of the causes. Likewise, pay attention when your partner(s) expresses or shows that they are uncomfortable with a sexual situation.

As you begin communicating with your partner, you will likely start to notice that boundaries aren't always clear cut. While sometimes boundaries are specific sexual activities that one needs to avoid, boundaries are also about noticing when a partner doesn't seem like themself or accepting when a partner just isn't in the mood. Boundaries can evolve and change, which is why it should never be assumed that what someone consented to in the past is what they will consent to in the present or future. You must continually communicate in order to have true consent.

Even after nearly a decade of having sex with each other, my husband and I are still learning more about each other's boundaries and desires. Some of our boundaries were easy for us to explain from the beginning, but other issues didn't reveal themselves until we had been together for years. Some boundaries have changed with time as our emotions and bodies are not stagnant things. The main thing that we've found works for us is that when one of us desires sex, we always make it clear that there is no obligation on the other person's part. This lack of pressure to have sex is what has helped me become much more comfortable and excited about sexual interactions. We know that when we have sex it is because we both want to.

Without going into all the details of my sex life, let me make one thing very clear, the myth that good consent ruins sex is so far from the truth. The exact opposite has been true for me. Sex between us only gets better the more we understand each other's preferences and boundaries.

When you allow yourself to share your boundaries with sexual partners, you are exploring your sexual desires because, by learning what doesn't work for you, you are also learning more about what does work for you. Without this kind of healthy exploration, you are likely not enjoying sex as much as you could or should. Open communication on boundaries is just the beginning of learning what is best for you and your partner(s) sexually. The more you communicate, the more you will understand what you and your partner(s) need in order to have a healthy sex life.

Reflection Questions

- What past interactions have made you feel uneasy, violated, and/or misunderstood?

- Are there certain things (e.g. images, sexual positions, graphic stories, etc.) that make you feel uncomfortable? What triggers negative emotions for you?

- If you or a partner have ignored a boundary in the past, what boundary was it? How did it affect you and your partner? Does this issue come up again and again? Or, was it an isolated incident?

- Do you need to utilize the help of outside resources?

- Do you feel comfortable communicating with your partner(s) about your sexual boundaries and desires?

- If you are currently in a sexual relationship, when was the last time you communicated with your partner(s) about sex? Have you checked-in with your partner(s) to see if there is anything about your sexual interactions that makes them uncomfortable?

Practice Action

Reflect on and write down your thoughts on your own sexual boundaries. Even if you don't have any specific boundaries in mind, simply write down your understanding of boundaries for yourself. Next, consider what you wrote and practice how you would turn your own reflections into a conversation with a sexual partner. Lastly, when you're ready, have a conversation about boundaries with a sexual partner.

Dilligence + Battlements

Kelly Powers

As a result of disability, I became a daily bus commuter for the first time at the age of 36. It was one of the most illuminating experiences in my life to watch how people behave around strangers, test boundaries, respect each other's time and privacy— employing various methods of deflection.

You see everything imaginable, from people willing to go to tremendous lengths to avoid any kind of interaction with a stranger to people who are equally entitled and will shoulder their way into a stranger's conversation. One day, a boy in his twenties asked me what my disability was. Receiving weekly reminders about my right to privacy and constantly reflecting on my own boundaries, I found the question to be rude, and so I told him that I'd rather not talk about it. To my surprise, he responded, "It's okay. I understand. Don't feel bad. I have a disability too. I am autistic. Do you know what that is?"

I know all too well about autism. I was diagnosed with it at the age of 32. It saddened me deeply that he referred to it as a disability, but it explained his lack of tact or respect for social mores. I can understand and respect why he'd bring it up to a stranger to chime in, "I'm sorry. I just can't help that I'm like this. I really do try."

You apologize a lot when you are autistic. Because of the history of eugenics in the US, autism wasn't properly incorporated into psychological manuals until the 1990s. By then, I was too old to be screened for it and since I've never had biological children to inherit it, I hadn't been screened for it—until I mentioned to the right therapist that I continually failed to notice people's nonverbal expressions of their boundaries. But I had done much damage to the relationships around me already before I received my diagnosis and had a roadmap to effective management.

Prior to my diagnosis, my therapist and I had been deadlocked for six months, without any real progress. She was always frustrated with me and would say things like, "You really have to do your part if you want this to work." And by that she meant that she didn't feel like I was spending time reflecting on and analyzing the nuances of the events of the previous week that resulted in conflict. I really tried. I would remember every bit of conflict that happened between our twice weekly two-hour appointments, but I had socially isolated myself and didn't always have that much conflict, so we instead spent months talking about every bit of hardship in my childhood, analyzing the ways that I'd been treated, how I was reserved with people now as a result, and how to handle better things that were under my own control and agency. At first, I was very much like a lost, wandering puppy, in desperate need of help to find resolution. She would frequently have to kick me out of our sessions saying, "You have to leave now" or "You have to give me money now." I would stumble out onto the street and wander through the rest of my day, trying to make sense of any of it.

I started working with her as a recently divorced 28-year-old, accused of emotionally abusing my ex over the course of a six-year relationship. This disruption and accusation destroyed my self-confidence and left me in a crumpled, emotional mess. I didn't want to hurt people, of course. And I was frankly lost as to how the situation had spiraled so badly out of control.

My ex had sent me a letter, which turned out to be our last communication. The recurring themes in it were about me failing to understand or hear her and my lack of understanding or respect for the importance of "little things." She was trying to tell me that I was missing—and thus violating—her boundaries. This theme continued to ring true throughout my therapy sessions.

Most of the reading said that an abusive personality should never be trusted, no effort should be put into rehabilitation, and I should be regarded as hopeless and a waste of time, given this accusation. I believe that all problems are solvable so I sought professional help. I had been in therapy before. I had even been in couple's therapy with my ex, where she made me swear never to tell our counselor that she was cheating on me. So this time felt different. My ex had demanded in her letter that I resolve issues stemming from my abusive upbringing through feminist counseling. This felt easily resolvable and even reasonable but utterly terrifying to revisit my childhood in intensive therapy. During the first two months of our sessions, my therapist tried and tried to get a rise out of me and evaluated how responsible I felt about my own actions. She concluded that I took responsibility for my actions and didn't point blame on other people for things that I had done. She felt that I did not exhibit traits of an abusive personality but that did not mean that our relationship was not abusive. I, thinking in terms of things in ones and zeroes, could not understand what any of this meant, and it confused me more.

I remember telling my therapist about the violence, intimidation, and conditional love around my growing up—identically recreated in my marriage—causing me to try to stay in the good graces of the people that I thought loved me. Eventually, at the end of one of our sessions, seemingly by chance, I mentioned that I could not ever see emotions by looking into people's faces. She explained to me that newborn babies can understand emotion and communication through nonverbal expression. My therapist seemed shocked, told me that it might indicate autism, that we'd revisit it next week, and kicked me out as I wondered why this had never come up before at any point in the past thirty years.

On the way home I realized that people probably had explained this to me—and likely many times—just not in the singular ways that I could understand. As upsetting as all of these compounding realizations were in the short term, it was far more edifying. For my entire life I'd had trouble making friends and relating beyond surface interactions. Many times I'd watch people exit my life without explanation, at least not one that I understood. They wanted me to pick up on "signs," or as far as I was concerned, it felt like they wanted me to be psychic.

This realization quickly took over my therapy sessions. For the next six months I remained lost. What did it mean? How did society work? Would I ever regain my confidence? Should I just move to a desert island? I was clumsily trying to please everyone around me but was instead continually misstepping and creating more hurt and conflict. A life of solitude seemed like the safest way to proceed. Life just felt like an ongoing downward spiral. In a world of neurotypical people being framed as "normal," it seemed best for me to disengage and cause less harm.

About the time I gave up on finding a happy and harmonious relationship, I met my current partner. She was aware of the dramas in my life and accepted me anyway, having much more understanding of the nuances of situations like these than other people that I was accustomed to. She was caring, could see my potential, listened closely, and was supportive of me but still pushed me to do better all the time and not just accept where I was at. She recognized effort and saw how difficult things were for me, yet how much I tried.

At that time, autism meant that I understood everything literally, and even now I have a hard time understanding nuances and jokes because of it. I feel things deeply and intensely and have a hard time showing empathy with others because I have a hard time understanding emotions that aren't my own. If I can relate someone's emotion to my own, I feel them very deeply, but it is often difficult to get to that point. I used to need to hear something said out loud in plain language to understand it. Boundaries are rarely expressed in plain language. And therein lies the problem. It's like how my therapist had to say, "You have to leave now" in

My therapist believes that very poor and incompatible communication habits partnered with missed boundaries can create a lot of mutual hurt. Those patterns and habits repeated daily could result in the same effects of relationship emotional abuse—to make it feel like a power struggle and to deeply impact the self-esteem of both parties.

In hindsight, I can recognize my ex reacting to feeling uncomfortable and the dynamics she was experiencing. She became physically violent towards me at times, everything became a tense negotiation, she began dating other people while we were married and would "punish" me when I didn't behave or communicate in the ways that she wanted. It was painful and scary, but it's now clear that from what she was experiencing, she was trying to get power back in the relationship. From what I gather, it seems that she felt expected or even obligated to go along with my decisions and that reacting in these ways felt like a reclamation of sorts. In one case, when my bicycle was stolen she saw it locked up on the street and rather than trying to get it returned to me, she simply took a photo and sent it to taunt me. Lack of communication and lack of understanding led her to feel as if she had been living under my rules and had to regain control, even as I remained oblivious to this dynamic.

A real example of this kind of dynamic is a neurotypical person who tells their autistic partner, "Don't let that man set foot on our property" so the autistic partner lays out boards for the visitor to walk on. For autistics, this is following orders to respect a partner's requests, but to most neurotypical people it's highly manipulative and doing what one wants in spite of a request. And the big problem is that despite autism, a person often has to co-exist with the rest of the world.

These revelations motivated me to understand my own predicament and see the situation outside the perspective of a single failed relationship. I could see the communication problems that I had been responsible for, and it was time to get my life under control. I spent a lot of my time reading and researching. I found that there are typically two kinds of people who have relationships with autistic individuals—other autistic people and

neurotypicals with bad boundaries. The former tend to resemble typical relationships on the inside, though habits tend to appear strange from the outside. The latter tend to be highly dysfunctional, and the neurotypical person tends to have their boundaries violated over and over by their autistic partner who has no idea that this is going on until everyone's patience is so exhausted that the relationship explodes into a bitter mess.

This was a very helpful piece of the puzzle as it explained how communication could devolve to such a degree that two different people in the same place were experiencing two very different things. At first, I took the position that it was the responsibility of others to accommodate my neurology. But this is a privileged position that only adds further strain onto others, and in reality, nobody was going to do that. I needed to be responsible for my own behavior—or at least meet people in the middle.

My comprehension of the situation became easier when I realized that both of my parents likely were autistic. They were born in the 1920s and 30s and were never diagnosed. For most of my life, I had found my mom to be very hard to deal with. She could almost never see my point of view, and it felt like she very much had to get her way, even though she likely did not see it that way. She would often lie to me in order to manipulate my behavior or understanding of a situation. This revelation about her maladaptive coping made it much easier to see what had likely been going on. She was saying how she felt and not hearing how I felt.

So I came around to a better, more moderated solution. If someone denies my experience of being autistic, I cease allowing them into my life. I share this detail about myself when I feel safe and comfortable, with some emotional history and proximity. Opening up to people is a risk, after all. For people who had known me for many years, it was hard for them to incorporate autism into the fabric of how they interpreted my personality and character. Many people said that they were "not surprised" but some people stridently denied it, often based on limited knowledge of autism or knowing an autistic person who functioned differently. If they had known me in my pre-teen years, I think they would have no doubts about it.

I can't go back and resolve a lifetime of confusing and hurtful interactions and relationships, but I was still in touch with most of the people I'd had serious relationships with, so I let each of them know, one by one, thinking that it might provide them with closure for what was likely a confusing and difficult situation. I accepted that even though I was neurologically different from most people, I still had the responsibility of being respectful, loving, and careful in my behavior and being accountable when I hurt someone.

Instead of a batterer program for abusers, I began cognitive-behavioral therapy, a program designed to teach autistic people how to interact with neurotypicals and recognize boundaries. I am an adult who is responsible for my own behavior, understanding it, and making changes so as to not negatively impact others. And with that, I've done my best. I've been re-trained in how to socialize healthfully and understand others' subtle communications and when someone might be expressing a boundary as well as upholding clear and enforceable boundaries of my own.

Fifteen years later, I've never been happier and have carved out a wonderful life by respecting other people's boundaries and defining my own. No amount of cognitive retraining can make me neurotypical, and I still make mistakes and do or say things that come across as callous, but these instances are reduced by 95 percent. I found a balance that isn't totally crippling to my functionality. I identified that in a relationship, I need to be trusted, supported, and respected. I've found that when any of these elements are missing, there is a quick and downward spiral that seemingly can't be recovered from. It's not always easy, of course, but my new blood pact with the world led to restored confidence, stronger socialization, and my first healthy relationship—of fifteen years.

I wish I'd had more time to discuss autism with the kid on the bus and tell him that it doesn't have to be a disability if he doesn't let it be one. Harnessed correctly, you can manage interactions in a world of people unlike you, to give and receive respect.

Types of Boundaries

- 👍 Physical
- 👕 Property
- 🔥 Sexual
- ❤️ Emotional-Relational
- ❄️ Intellectual
- 🙏 Spiritual
- ⏰ Time

Unf*ck Your BOUNDARIES

Written by Dr. Faith G Harper
Designed by Linette Lanei

Attachment Styles

aka How we do relationships

high avoidance

Dismissing-avoidant

Fearful avoidant

Low anxiety

High Anxiety

Secure

Preoccupied

low avoidance

fMRI shows the amygdala *lights up* at personal space violations *even* when conscious cues weren't PRESENT!

Gut Reactions are real, (litera) things

Try Communicating what you DO want rather than what you DON'T

I feel _____
when you _____
what I want is _____

Communicating Boundaries and needs

Types of communication

1. What I mean to say
2. What I actually say
3. What the other person hears
4. What the other person thinks you mean

High Conflict Personalities

Characteristics

1. Limited emotional self-control
2. Limited Behavioural self-control
3. Black and White thinking
4. Externalising

Communicate using BIFF

Brief
Informative
Friendly
Firm

Avoid the 3 A's

Advice
Admonishment
Apologies

When communication breaks down...

Beware of Coercive Control
But it is Fixable!

Pane of Glass method

Imagine a pane of Glass shielding you.

Grey rock method
Be as boring and unresponsive as a grey rock

CHAPTER 5: EMBRACING CONSENT

Our family, race, sexuality, gender, health, personal history, and all of the various components that make us who we are—they all contribute to how we understand consent. These various parts that make up the whole of our identity influence how comfortable we feel in different situations, including sexual interactions. Hence, what makes me comfortable during sex won't be the same as what makes other people comfortable. We all have different needs when it comes to consensual sexual situations.

From Pressure to Assault

In my first three years of sexual activity, I thought it was much simpler than that. My idea of a lack of consent was physically forced sexual assault. I didn't understand that coercion and pressure in sexual situations are also not consent. I knew that I felt uncomfortable in certain situations, but I just thought I had a low sex drive. I assumed that men always wanted sex more than women did, so I thought it was normal that my boyfriend would pressure me into sex. But, while the experience

of being pressured into sex may be common, it shouldn't be normal, and it definitely isn't healthy.

The pressure of sex with a partner makes it difficult for many people to say either "yes" or "no." Untangling your own internal wants from another person's requests is tricky. When I was with my ex-boyfriend, I noticed that the mood of sex switched for me at some point because of the pressure that I felt from him. I became a resentful gatekeeper for the sex that he wanted. Many of the interactions are foggy in my recollections, but I remember the feelings. As noted, we would often be drunk or angry. I noticed my bodily reactions often corresponded with my comfort level.

One sexual interaction with my ex-boyfriend, however, remains clear in my memory. I will unfortunately always remember the time that I verbally said no. He was behind me, and I was on all fours. As previously mentioned, I struggled with pain in this position. In this specific interaction, the sex was becoming more and more physically painful so I asked him to stop. Yet he continued. I ultimately literally pushed him off me to end the interaction.

I think this interaction is imprinted in my mind because it was the closest thing I had experienced to my previous understanding of sexual assault. The moment resembled assault to me because he continued having sex with me after I had said no. At this time, my only reference for sexual assault was the crimes that I had seen reported in the news. Rape meant a stranger attacking a young white woman sexually despite her struggle and resistance. I still wasn't able to recognize my own experience with sexual assault, but I felt its effects. I was extremely preoccupied with rape in a destructive way. I felt that at some point in my life I was going to be raped.

I didn't realize that I was fearing something that is uncommon (stranger rape), while experiencing something that is very common—sexual coercion from a partner. Although the instance described above is imprinted in my brain, there were many other times when I technically said "yes" that weren't consensual. These other times blend together and are foggy—memory is a funny thing when it comes to emotional trauma, but all of those moments contributed to an overwhelming distrust of my boyfriend and men in general.

He wasn't the first man to take advantage of me when I was drinking. Right before I started dating him, I had gotten drunk with a few friends at one of their houses. One was a close friend from high school, and we had been on a couple dates. I was drunk, like falling-over drunk, yet he led me upstairs where we had sex. I vaguely remember saying no, but I was so drunk that there is no way I can really verify what happened, and I definitely wasn't capable of consenting to sex. I had previously had sober sex with him, a fact that no doubt would have been used against me if I had ever pursued legal charges against him. I also know that at that time, in 2008, before consent had become a mainstream topic of discussion, this "friend" had no clue that what he did was wrong or that it affected me at all. This is not to make excuses for him—he should've been a better person—but this kind of experience was normalized at the time. Some people are still raised thinking that there is nothing wrong with this kind of interaction, which is a huge problem when it comes to ensuring consent in sexual relationships.

Through all of this, I assumed that my fear of rape was irrational and my responsibility to manage. Because external influences often pointed to this male-female dynamic of men wanting sex and women resisting it as a normal part of life, I thought something was wrong with me when I started having issues with the sexual dynamics of my relationships. I discontinued my friendship with the "friend" who assaulted me, and I eventually broke up with my ex-boyfriend, leaving behind the toxic sexual dynamics with him. But even then, I did not directly relate these interactions to sexual assault. I left these relationships because I felt trapped and insecure, but I continued to feel vulnerable to sexual assault.

Learning about Consent

I decided to sign up for a self-defense class. In the first portion of the class, we talked about consent as the act of saying "yes!" to sex. In my insecure state, this insight initially made me feel like once again there was something wrong with me. I had sometimes felt violated even if I had agreed to sex. My boundaries had still been crossed somehow. These situations usually involved a "yes" borne out of obligation or pressure from my ex-boyfriend. The more we spoke about verbal

consent in the self-defense course, however, I began to connect the dots. I started to realize that my fear of sexual assault, initially triggered by news sources emphasizing the rape of young girls, had been exacerbated by the sexual obligation that my boyfriend had imposed on me. I finally recognized that my boyfriend had exerted control over my body. I grasped a new understanding of sexual assault and how it is more often inflicted by someone who knows the victim.

My situation was far from the most extreme situations of sexual abuse and trauma, but little by little the unhealthy sexual dynamics of my relationship had chipped away at an already damaged understanding of healthy sexual relationships. The situations that lead to unhealthy relationships are often subtle. Anytime you have a lack of respect for a person's autonomy—sexually, physically, or emotionally—you're limiting consent within a relationship. You're making it more difficult for that person to say no, which is an especially easy trap to fall into when people are emotionally attached to one another in a relationship.

We must all work to understand when a sexual situation is not consensual. We must recognize the personhood of the people we hurt and take responsibility when we cross boundaries in subtle ways through pressure and emotional influence. Consent can only truly be given in a safe environment and sober state of mind. Nothing, whether alcohol, privilege, or another corrupted tool of power, should be used to blur consent because nothing should prevent a person from making decisions about their own sexual interactions. Assuming or ignoring consent is an abuse of power.

Consent is about so much more than just saying yes or no. When I felt violated with my ex-boyfriend, it was because I wasn't in an environment where I felt safe expressing my wants. Disregard, pressure, intimidation, or manipulation can all lead to an unsafe and uncomfortable environment where consent is not possible. In any intimate interaction, all parties should feel like they can communicate their desires. Consent is about respecting each other and creating environments where people feel comfortable.

Creating Safe Spaces

Discussions within Communities and with Sexual Partners

You might be thinking that's all great, but how do we create environments where people feel comfortable? We need to talk about "it." You know, "doing it," "making love," "fucking," and my least favorite, "getting lucky." Looking at these sexual euphemisms already gives us an idea of what we're up against. Our words can evoke romance, vulgarity, passivity. "Getting lucky" is my least favorite because sex should never be about luck. Consensual sex is a mutual decision.

Verbal and visual ideas of sex will always exist in mainstream culture, but clear discussions about healthy relationships, sexuality, and gender are much harder to find. Even within progressive circles, these are issues that need to be considered when we interact with each other sexually. We need to take action to learn and teach more about healthy sexual interactions. We are all responsible for creating an environment of consent, which means communicating with one another. Here are just a few examples of the things that we should be talking about:

Discussion Questions for Communities

- What is the difference between sexual orientation and gender?

- What kinds of relationships exist besides heterosexual monogamous relationships?

- How are sexual relationships affected by power and privilege?

- What media, entertainment, situations, experiences, etc. have influenced our ideas of enjoyable sex?

- What do I do if I unintentionally cross someone's boundaries in a sexual relationship?

Discussion Questions for Partners and Close Friends

- Do you feel comfortable talking about sex with your partner(s)? If not, why?

- Do you feel comfortable having sex with your partner(s)? If not, why?

- What kind of relationship (open, monogamous, polyamorous, etc.) are you looking for, if any?

- How do you and your partner(s) view gender and sexuality?

- Do you and/or your partner(s) identify as a specific gender (woman, man, nonbinary, etc.) and/or sexual orientation (straight, gay, bisexual, etc.)?

- What is your and your partner(s)' ideal sexual experience?

- What are your boundaries and what are your partner(s)' boundaries? Are you and your partner(s)' boundaries and preferences in conflict with one another?

When discussing these issues as a community, begin broadly. Discover how your friends and family view gender and sexual orientation. To start, do your family and friends understand that there is a difference between gender and sexual orientation? Many people are gaining a better grasp on the difference between how a person identifies (gender) and who they are attracted to (sexual orientation), but it never hurts to revisit the topic. There have been large changes in how we talk about gender and sexuality in a relatively short period of time. Rather than leave people who don't understand in the dust, it can be helpful to revisit these concepts that more progressive circles now take for granted.

I have had many people express to me a misunderstanding of genders outside of the traditional binary of men and women. I am honest with them that it takes time to understand. Virtually every single one of us has been socialized into the same binary system from birth, but the important thing is that we must try to understand that there are alternative ways of understanding gender. The acceptance of gender as a spectrum rather than a binary is crucial to the mental health and safety of so many of our fellow humans. If we don't make it clear that all genders are accepted, regardless of labels, we leave those who don't fit into the traditional binary vulnerable to hate crimes and insecurities.

Believe it or not, it is possible for people and societal ideas to change. Consent as a necessity in sexual relationships was just beginning to become a topic of conversation when I started writing the first edition of *Consensuality* in 2012 and now, a decade later, the idea of consent in sexual interactions is common knowledge. Of course, there's also a

backlash to that increase in knowledge. There will always be people who don't want to move forward, but thankfully, if you're reading this book, you're likely willing to have those conversations about consent in your relationships. You are one more person working towards a greater understanding of gender, sexuality, and consent. Most importantly, you are one less person going out into the world and hurting people because of a refusal to attempt understanding. It all comes down to caring for and respecting one another.

We should stretch the boundaries of each other's knowledge. Don't try to logically separate out all of the various components of gender, sexuality, and consent. Embrace that these topics are messy and complicated, that they require discussion, particularly in intimate relationships. If you state how you feel honestly and are open to these discussions, you'll begin diving into the many layers of healthy and consensual relationships with all kinds of people of different genders and sexualities.

In specific sexual relationships, the first place to go to with questions about sex is to the person/

people involved in the interaction. The communal conversation, however, should have begun long before that. Community education on sex needs to allow for discussion. If students and community members can't ask questions, sex ed becomes stagnant and limited to the current authority's view of sex. Don't mistake this for an excuse to run up to any person you want and ask them for details on their sex life. Currently, too much of the burden is on people who don't fit into the traditional straight cisgender view of the world. We always expect people who have found the courage to be themselves to then also explain all of the intimate details of their life to society. But, we all should be having these conversations in the appropriate environments, including in sex ed.

As of 2022, 29 states and DC require sexual education in public schools. Only ten states and DC require inclusive information on sexual orientation to be included in sexual education. Five states—Florida, Illinois, Louisiana, Mississippi, and Texas—actually require homosexuality to be described in negative terms if it is mentioned and/or for heterosexuality to be emphasized in a positive manner. Information on consent doesn't fare much

better when it comes to sexual education. Eleven states plus DC require consent to be included in sexual education. In the US, we've only made limited progress towards more comprehensive sex education programs.

We will likely continue to struggle amongst ourselves when it comes to legislating sexual education. In regards to official sex ed curriculum and other aspects of education, people are still actively attempting to restrict conversations about sexuality and gender. Florida's infamous "Don't Say Gay" law is an unfortunate example of what happens when people who don't understand gender and sexuality obtain power. And, each year, I'm sadly never surprised when the American Library Association's Most Challenged Books List is filled with books on gender and sexuality. We will never have healthy sexual interactions if we can't have open and honest discussions about gender and sexuality. So, while we have limited control over which laws are passed, we should do everything we can to normalize talking about gender and sexuality. We should talk to our partners. We should talk to our family. We should talk to our kids. When sex ed falls short, we should seek opportunities to fill in the gaps.

Embracing the Spectrum

In my own sexual education, I found that gender was the missing component. When presenting the female or male anatomy, my sexual education teachers ignored all of the different kinds of people that are connected to sexual organs. The unspoken assumption was that a male-bodied person would act like a "man" and a female-bodied person would act like a "woman." These days, people are more accepting that things aren't that simple, but sex ed in K-12 schools is still lagging behind. The focus has always been on preventing pregnancy, and while a very important component, pregnancy is not the only important topic when it comes to sex. Sex ed should be about so much more than reproduction.

One of my college professors encouraged us to create our own gender spectrum. She drew a line on the board with the female symbol on the right side and the male symbol on the left side. She asked us to write actions on the board in the correct location of the spectrum. Our actions ranged from "brushing teeth," placed in the middle

of the spectrum, to "painting nails" and "playing football" on opposite sides of the board. None of the actions had to do with a person's biological sex, rather they matched our cultural perceptions of the gender binary: women and men.

After we had created our gender spectrum on the board, she asked us to place ourselves on the spectrum. A clump of women marked their spots just to the right of center, indicating that they leaned only slightly towards "feminine." One male and a few females placed themselves in the exact center of the spectrum. The remaining men lingered just to the left of center, indicating that they only leaned slightly towards "masculine." A few females joined these men, crossing the gender divide to place themselves on the "masculine" side of the spectrum despite perceptions of their identity. Only a small percentage of the class was scattered at the ends of the spectrum, identifying as either fully "masculine" or fully "feminine." Most of us clung to gender neutrality, preferring to disconnect our identities from our perceived genders. My professor pointed out how it was less likely for men to recognize publicly if they felt "feminine," which was exemplified by the complete lack of men on the "feminine" side of the spectrum, but she also recognized that each year more students migrated to the middle of the spectrum.

While emotions weren't on the spectrum that my classmates and I communally created in the course, they are just as equally misplaced into gendered categories as actions. We often tell women that they will become attached to their partner after sex and will desire exclusive relationships, while men are viewed as being prone to polygamy and able to have sex without emotional ties. The myth of an emotional gender divide (which I sincerely hope is becoming less common) perpetuates itself in conservative environments where people are less open to conversations about sex. However, this divide between men and women is just one of many narratives in people's sexual experiences. There is no primary narrative for any category of people because ultimately the categories themselves are arbitrary. The important part of allowing feelings and emotions to become a part of the discussion about sex is that it allows us to see that sexual experiences are diverse, emotionally and physically.

Even a spectrum that places "feminine" and "masculine" on opposite ends is becoming increasingly outdated, as characteristics given to these categories are often based on the values of traditional cisgender marriages and relationships. The binary of men and women in the absence of other options inherently discourages people from expressing feelings and ideas that fit outside of those categories. Expanding outside of the categories of men and women is long overdue in the United States. Before nonbinary was even a thought in American culture, people in other countries were already incorporating systems outside of our traditional gender binary into their communities. In many cultures, there is a third gender. Research tombois in West Sumatra and Fa'afafine in Samoa to discover just two of the many genders existing in the world. You'll be amazed by the variety of gender expressions that go beyond a person's biological sex, including nonbinary, a gender identity that more and more people are discovering better represents them.

Culturally acceptable gender categories outside of man and woman can sometimes create safer environments for people who are not cisgender, yet too often people who aren't cisgender are still treated as second-class citizens. Ultimately, until we can completely rid ourselves of the traditional gender binary, there will be judgment and sometimes violence towards people who don't fit into the neat but false categories of man and woman.

So do yourself a favor and start talking and listening to your partner(s). Don't assume that you know where they fall on a gendered spectrum. Your partner(s)' gender and sexuality, along with your own gender and sexuality, are likely more complex and nuanced than you could have ever imagined.

Reflection Questions

- How do you express consent in your sexual interactions? Likewise, how do you determine the consent of your partner?

- What was your sexual education experience like?

- Are you able to speak openly about gender and sexuality with your

partner(s) and/or friends? If not, think about why and how you might start some conversations.

Practice Action

Ask your partner(s) or a close friend what their sexual education experience was like. Discuss what was included and/or what was missing from your and your partner(s) sexual education experiences. Use this as an opportunity to talk about how your conceptions of consent, gender, and sexuality formed. You'll both likely gain insights into each other's views on these topics and areas where your sexual education fell short.

If you choose to talk to a sexual partner for this practice action, this is also an opportunity to discuss consent, gender, and sexuality in regards to your own sexual interactions.

THE FINAL CO-ADVENTURER:
You!

There are many factors that can complicate consent in relationships. Views of gender and sexuality, socialization, trauma, emotions, and many other things influence and complicate our interactions. Navigating these topics and communicating openly about these issues is a great start to forming healthy relationships, but what keeps consent going long term within relationships? It takes a commitment from you, me, all of us, to prioritize consent in our relationships. The following three exercises will become your own personal roadmap for sustaining consent within your relationships. Although I've included my own examples for the exercises below, ultimately *Consensuality* is your opportunity to invent your own narrative of consent. Take out a journal and start exploring the following exercises on your own. Recognize your own growth, but also hold yourself accountable. This is only the beginning; continue to revisit these exercises as needed.

The process of creating healthy connections (including sex) never ends, so it is crucial to ensure that we sustain healthy habits. Use all of the thoughts, feelings, and ideas that you've explored

in *Consensuality* to envision, create, and maintain your own map towards healthy relationships.

Writing Exercise 1: Revisit your starting point by once again recognizing your own influences. What roles were you socialized into? What roles did you choose for yourself? What antiquated views or ideas have you supported, intentionally or unintentionally, in your life?

Express how your perspective shapes your values. In addition, if you have a sexual partner(s) ask them if they would feel comfortable completing this exercise as well. This exercise will help you build awareness of how denying your own perspective or disregarding someone else's perspective can create barriers for consent.

Helen's Example:

> What I wanted fifteen years ago came straight out of a cheesy romance novel: tall, dark, and handsome. I was focused on finding the "perfect" man, but I was disappointed when many men, who appeared to be the ideal rom-com love interest, had antiquated views of dating

and sex. I had to reimagine what I actually wanted and not what I had been socialized into.

Every day, I hope to recognize and challenge the abuse that many people experience in sexual relationships because of gender stereotypes, but there are still some barriers in my way. Despite societal progress, I sometimes feel limits on my emotions, my appearance, and my physical movement. I challenge these limits by moving freely without fear of physical harm. I feel confident within my own relationships. I strive for my relationships to be free of gender stereotypes. I express what I want during sexual interactions I choose to abandon the shame and resentment that I felt for years.

I understand that there are limits to my perspective. I am white, which gives me a huge amount of privilege in this world. It can be hard to see past that sometimes, but it is far from impossible. I grew up without realizing that white women have been

placed on a protective pedestal throughout the history of the world. One of the things I want to recognize for myself now is how this privilege often creates blindspots in my interactions, making it more crucial for me to listen to people of other racial and social backgrounds.

Exercise 2: What mistakes have you made in the past? Be honest! This is just for you! How can you learn from the mistakes and form healthy habits moving forward?

Forming healthy relationships includes expressing your values to others, but it is crucial to examine our actions along the way to ensure that we aren't trampling over other people in the process.

Helen's Example:

Even after talking about gender, sexuality, and consent with the people in my life, I still encountered bumps in the road, and there have been times where my actions didn't coincide with my beliefs. I've struggled with sex when alcohol is involved. My problem was binge drinking. Once I went over an edge, all my hard-earned work on myself went out the window. I am now aware that all of my impulses towards self-destruction and unhealthy habits are amplified by alcohol.

My husband and I have worked on it together, and we now know to be cautious when either of us has had even one drink. We've both expressed these concerns with one another and have established boundaries when it comes to drinking and sex. These days I avoid binge drinking. This change was absolutely necessary for me to maintain healthy relationships. My husband and I will steer clear of sex if there is any question of the other person's intoxication. I know too much alcohol has a way of bringing out my old issues, and it isn't worth the risk for me.

Exercise 3: Finally, combine it all to write a love note about your own personal boundaries for your future relationships. Reinvent love as the respect and consent that you plan to experience with your current or future sexual partner(s).

Writing a love note for yourself and your current or future sexual partners may feel strange. Love notes are usually cheesy and silly, but this is a different kind of love note. In this love note, you will take a deep dive into your current situation and what you need in order to have consensual relationships. There are reasons to be fearful or unsure, but there are also so many reasons to express ourselves. In this love note for yourself and your future/current sexual partner(s), you will express your commitment to building healthy relationships.

Helen's Example:

Dear Us,

My love stories have been spouted out of me, as gossip, as threats, as ramblings, but the following letter is my record of my true love, a love that means respect for myself and others.

I often used the word "crazy" in matters of love. You (in this case, my husband) and I started dating after a particularly "crazy" and unhealthy relationship. "Crazy" was normal for me, which felt like a barrier to us obtaining a mutual sense of our feelings for one another. I didn't know what to expect when we started dating, but I knew from experiences in past relationships that I didn't want to be with someone who would restrict me. I had to fall completely for us as partners, not just for you. I had to know that we wouldn't control each other through our interactions together whether it was conscious manipulation or just the way it played out in practice.

I wanted to be with someone who was considerate. I was ready to work towards respecting one another in a mutually consenting relationship. What I didn't know was that looking for positive and free communication with another person would create an intense love. I discovered that this seemingly shy boy could be a magnificent and somewhat scary creature. Your ten toes were dotted with homemade ink to spell out your spontaneity. You moved uncontrollably at dance parties. You had glimpses of freedom in your actions. But I mistakenly compared our freedom with one another to my past feelings of "crazy."

I thought all I could feel was "crazy," yet we hadn't crossed a boundary or restricted one another in any way. We felt incredibly free in the relationship. The thing I realize now is that it is difficult to express, feel and sustain freedom. As much as we've all heard that phrase, "just be yourself" again and again, society hasn't actually provided us with that opportunity. The influences of stereotypes and unhealthy expectations rear their heads in our interactions with lovers. Communication can deteriorate into awkward and painful misunderstandings when partners are holding back or just poorly matched. But communication turned into freedom when we started expressing ourselves respectfully.

It took time for us to completely reveal ourselves to one another. In fact, we ended up needing time away from each other along the way. We were evolving into more honest and open people. Initially, we rarely reflected on how our past experiences were still influencing our connection to one another. But after diving into consensuality on my own, I had an open conversation with you about a subject that I had never felt comfortable discussing. I had stumbled upon an article stating that the best rape prevention was for women to stop getting drunk. It was an emotional trigger for me considering my complicated past with alcohol and sex. Articles that unfairly blamed and stereotyped victims made me afraid to recognize my own experiences with sexual coercion and assault.

A few nights prior, our friends had also talked about an instance when a woman had sexually assaulted you years before we her. You had previously had sex with this woman and regretted it. When you saw her a second time, you asked your friends to ensure that you were not left alone with her. After an outing to a park and many drinks, you all returned to a friend's house, but the woman told you to stay in the car and then proceeded to sexually assault you despite you asking her to stop multiple times. As our friends recounted the story, they laughed. They wrote it off as a drunken mistake. I felt bad that this traumatic experience had been turned into a joke. I wanted you to know that I would understand if you wanted to talk about what happened.

We had never thoroughly discussed the topic, but I knew that I wanted both of us to know that we were safe in our relationship. I wanted to acknowledge that a non-consensual sexual interaction, even if it is with a previous sexual partner or under the influence of alcohol, is sexual assault and not the fault of the victim. Talking about sexual assault was scary for both of us. I thought you weren't acknowledging our experiences, and you thought that I was mad because you previously hadn't considered consent in this way.

Thankfully, all that was required for us to work through our fears was respectful communication. Issues that could've festered and ruined us if we had kept them from one another actually brought us closer to each other. We talked about our experiences and how they affected us. The conversation is ultimately what led to our realization that even if we usually felt like sex under the influence of alcohol was fine between us, it was problematic to think that it would always be okay. What if there was a night in the future when one of us didn't want to have sex, but wasn't capable of saying "no" under the influence of alcohol? We decided that day to avoid sex when either of us was drinking because sex is never worth the possibility of violating one another. This was an important

boundary that we established together by recognizing that we each also had our own pasts and related boundaries.

Anytime we hurt one another or recognize the potential of hurting one another, we have an open discussion to resolve the issue together. We won't be able to foresee every risk, but it's liberating to know that we can talk about any topic and find a resolution that works for both of us. The discussions are our means of understanding and maintaining what consent means to us. No one knows what the future holds, but no matter what, I'm eternally grateful to us for prioritizing consent and health for ourselves.

With love and consent,

Helen

To continue patterns of consent, continue to check in with yourself and your sexual partners. The work does not end here! In the final pages of this book, consider the healthy tools of communication that you currently use and your own goals for increasing consent within your relationships. Express yourself, but also remember to listen. Ask questions, kindly and respectfully. Check in with each other by asking simple questions, such as "How are you doing?" "Does this feel good to you?" "Are you comfortable with this?" We take these questions for granted when we feel like we know our sexual partner, but people are complex. People change and hopefully grow. You may think you know yourself and your sexual partners, but if you don't stop and reflect, you can't guarantee a thorough understanding of the intricacies and concerns within your relationships. It is impossible to establish and respect boundaries without talking to one another.

People are often cautious when communicating about relationships because it doesn't always work out, but that doesn't have to be a bad thing. We're taught that we will be saved by a knight in shining armor or that we will rescue a princess at the end of the story. If you are not that knight or that princess—and make no mistake, virtually none of us are—you'll feel forgotten until you realize that you get to write your own narrative. When it comes to sex, consent, companionship, and any other aspect of human connections, each relationship is its own unique set of interactions. What works for you, may not work for other people and vice versa.

The journey toward understanding consent opens up many options for how you can express your own version of consensuality in relationships. When you establish clear lines of communication with another person, an intense and respectful bond should develop. If your relationship goes the opposite direction, it's time to let go and move on. You should feel comfortable saying yes, no, or anything else that you feel in the moment, and your sexual partners should feel the same way.

I wouldn't have been able to find respect for myself and my own sexual partner without the process of finding my consensuality. The experience has helped me feel confident in our ability as people to create healthy and respectful relationships. I feel empowered by all of the voices that choose consent in their relationships, and I

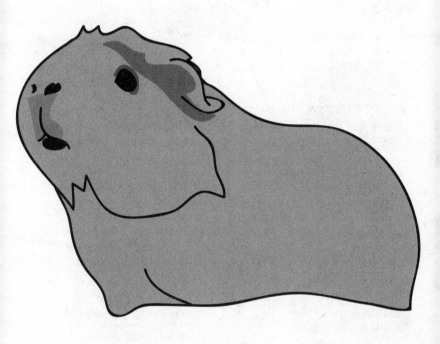

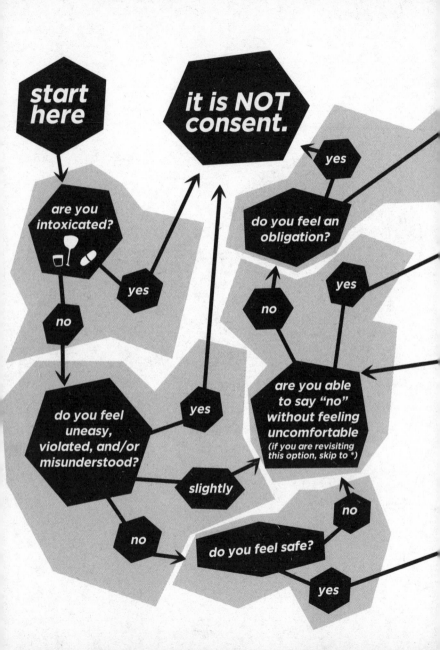

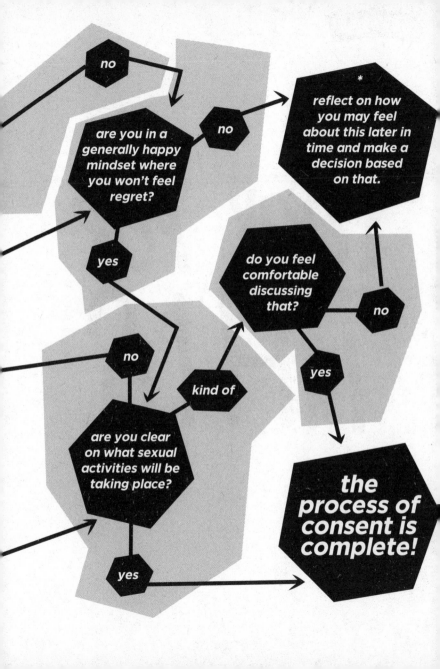

LOOK FOR THIS

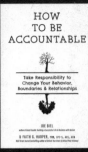

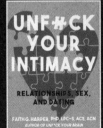